Japan and the United States:

Fifty Years of Partnership

JAPAN AND
THE UNITED STATES

Fifty Years of Partnership

Edited by Chihiro Hosoya
and A50 Editorial Committee

The Japan Times

First edition: August 2001

Published by The Japan Times, Ltd.
4-5-4 Shibaura, Minato-ku, Tokyo 108-0023, Japan
Phone: +81-3-3453-2013
Fax: +81-3-3453-8023

Cover design: CADEC

Printed in Japan
ISBN4-7890-1061-9

Contents

FOREWORD

YOSHIO OKAWARA
President, A50 Executive Committee

September 8, 2001, marks the 50th anniversary of the signing in San Francisco of the peace treaty whereby Japan was freed from the yoke of the occupation and was allowed to rejoin the international community. In the latter half of the 20th century, Japan achieved remarkable success by the strenuous efforts of the entire nation and became the second-largest economy in the world, but it was there and then, in San Francisco 50 years ago, that this entire process started.

In the devastation following the war, a dejected public mind and social disorder plagued the nation, and the economy was in utter ruin. Aid from the United States, both official and nongovernmental, saved the Japanese people from starvation and prevented the spread of diseases. The assistance included the Government and Relief in Occupied Areas (GARIOA) and Economic Rehabilitation Account for Occupied Areas (EROA) programs, as well as relief supplies financed by private goodwill contributions. Many Japanese fondly remember school lunches of powdered milk and bread that were gifts from the Cooperative for American Relief to Everywhere (CARE) and the Licensed Agency for Relief of Asia (LARA.)

It was through the strong support of the United States that a peace treaty was worked out rather early, even though the circumstances necessitated a prompt settlement with Japan so as to solidify the West as the Cold War with the East intensified. Neither can we overlook the U.S. help and cooperation in subsequently securing Japan's membership in the United Nations, International Monetary Fund, World Bank, and General Agreement on Tariffs and Trade, which enabled Japan to surmount the handicap of being a defeated nation and thereby to establish a foothold for doing its share as a democracy in the international community.

Thanks to our alliance with the United States—based on the bilateral Security Treaty that was entered into together with the peace treaty—serving as the cornerstone of our foreign relations, we have enjoyed peace and prosperity throughout the postwar years. During this time we have been able to carry out brisk reconstruction and to follow the path of high economic growth through access to the giant and relatively open market of the United States and the introduction of large amounts of capital from that country.

During the past 50 years there arose incidents that could have shaken the alliance. These included the turmoil in Japan over the 1960 revision of the security treaty, the so-called Nixon shocks in the early 1970s, and our clumsy response to the Gulf War of 1991. After the late 1960s, as Japan's economy expanded, bilateral trade disputes, such as the textile feud and the controversy over automobiles, often turned into serious strains. But deepening interdependence between the two countries enabled them to unravel the occasional tangles through mutual efforts, so much so that the United States came to recognize that its "ties with Japan are the most important bilateral relationship in the world," as declared by Mike Mansfield when he was the U.S. ambassador to Tokyo.

On the occasion of the 50th anniversary of the signing of the San Francisco Peace Treaty, our group of like-minded citizens is conducting a grassroots campaign, titled the A50 Project, with a call for "developing the 50 years of appreciation into 50 years of trust." By this endeavor on the basis of our recognition of the historic facts as described above, we hope to express our gratitude in a clear-cut manner to the United States and its people for the support they extended to us, and to help cement a solid relationship, bonded in mutual trust, with the United States at a time when ties between the two countries are bound to be increasingly important as the 21st century progresses.

The A50 Project mainly consists of providing scholarships for young American scholars, sending a caravan delegation to approximately 30 U.S. states for the purpose of interchange at the grassroots level, and of publishing a book on the 50 years of postwar Japan–U.S. relations.

Written in Japanese and titled *Japan and the United States—50 Years of Partnership*, the book was conceived to provide a general audience with expert views on how the postwar Japan–U.S. relationship evolved, what it means to Japan, and what approaches we should consider for the future. This English version comprises some complete as well as some abridged translations of certain articles in the Japanese edition, along with certain original writings, and it is being published so as to contribute to American readers' understanding of our bilateral ties.

It gives us in the A50 Executive Committee great pleasure that the book has been compiled under the general editorship of Dr. Chihiro Hosoya, professor emeritus of the International University of Japan, and that it includes contributions from authorities on political, diplomatic, economic, social, and cultural affairs. We extend our special thanks to the members of the editorial panel, who, despite the claims of busy lives, held many meetings to carefully develop ideas before completing their works.

Last, but not least, we also extend our sincere thanks to Mr. Toshiaki Ogasawara, chairman of The Japan Times, Ltd., for its valuable expert advice and assistance.

Chapter 1

JAPAN AND THE UNITED STATES:
A Half-Century of Partnership

TADASHI ARUGA*

1. THE OCCUPATION AND THE PEACE SETTLEMENT

At the end of World War II, defeated Japan was subject to the Allied Occupation. For the Japanese people, this occupation turned out to be a blessing in disguise. It was fortunate for them that the Allied occupation of Japan was for all practical purposes an American occupation. Under the occupation, the people of Japan were able to have peace, food, and an opportunity to reconstruct the country as a peaceful, democratic nation. Unlike Germany, Japan was allowed to maintain a unitary Japanese government supervised by the General Headquarters (GHQ) headed by General Douglas MacArthur, the Supreme Commander of the Allied Powers. Under his leadership, this country was able to undergo rather smoothly a

---

*   This English overview of Japan–U.S. relations since 1945 is an abridged translation of a much-longer historical survey of Japan–U.S. relations written in Japanese for *Nihon to Amerika: pātonāshippu no 50-nen* (Japan Times, 2001). The survey was jointly authored by Akira Iikura (the Occupation Period), Chihiro Hosoya (the 1950s and 1960s), Osamu Ishii (the 1970s and 1980s), and Tadashi Aruga (the 1990s). Although this English essay is based on the Japanese original, this writer has used his discretion rather liberally in editing it. He therefore takes full responsibility for this English version. He would like to thank Chihiro Hosoya, the editor of this volume, for correcting factual errors in proofs.

drastic transformation from a militaristic, authoritarian wartime country to a liberal, democratic postwar country. Emperor Hirohito and postwar Japanese leaders willingly cooperated with the occupation authorities in this transformation. Generally speaking, American soldiers were well-disciplined and American officials were persons of integrity. They provided the occupied nation with good governance. Thus, many friendships developed between the occupiers and the occupied people, and these became the human basis for postwar cooperative U.S.–Japan relations.

The original purposes of the occupation were the demilitarization and democratization of Japan. The welfare of the Japanese people was not considered a particular concern of the occupation authorities. But MacArthur and his staff soon understood that the occupation could not succeed if the supreme commander failed to help the Japanese people enjoy the most basic freedom, that is, freedom from hunger. In 1945, the Japanese rice harvest was very poor because of bad weather, resulting in an acute shortage of food in the defeated nation by early 1946. MacArthur promptly acted to meet this crisis. The GHQ released surplus food from the stocks of the U.S. army and secured emergency foodstuff exports from the United States. In 1946, 545,000 tons of grain and 142,000 tons of canned food were shipped to Japan pursuant to a relief program for the occupied countries.

MacArthur assured Prime Minister Shigeru Yoshida that no Japanese would starve as long as he was the supreme commander, and this episode and his food-relief activities endeared him very much to the Japanese. It should also be remembered that more than one million Americans donated funds for sending foodstuffs and other necessities to Japan through the Licensed Agencies for Relief in Asia (LARA) program, supported by a coalition of religious and nonreligious civic organizations.

Because Japan lacked money to import food and other necessities from abroad, the U.S. government continued to help Japan import them through the Government Appropriation for Relief in Occupied Areas (GARIOA) program. It was necessary for the United States to encourage Japan's economic recovery and to let Japan stand for itself if it hoped to reconstruct Japan as a stable democratic nation.

The policy of encouraging Japan's economic recovery was accelerated by the development of the Cold War. The United States, when it reviewed the East Asian situation, began to regard Japan, the only Asian country that had succeeded in industrializing itself before World War II, as a U.S. asset in the Cold War in Asia. Besides, the Chinese Nationalists were losing the civil war in China to the Communists. Democratized Japan therefore seemed to be the only country that could be a valuable ally of America in Asia. Accordingly, in 1948 the purpose of the occupation shifted to promoting Japan's economic recovery and political stability before a peace settlement with this country. Under the Economic Rehabilitation in Occupied Areas (EROA) program, the United States began to promote Japan's economic recovery by enabling Japan to purchase materials for industrial production.

Although it is not easy to calculate exactly how much aid Japan received from the United States during the occupation period, the total sum is estimated to be more than $2 billion. However, the Japan–U.S. agreement of 1962 that settled the GARIOA-EROA debts required Japan to repay only $490 million, approximately one-quarter of the total sum that the United States had provided, and the United States agreed to allocate most of the repayment money to development assistance and to use a portion of it to promote cultural exchanges between the two nations. In accordance with this agreement, the United States later founded the Japan-United States Friendship Commission in Washington to support bilateral cultural-exchange programs.

Nonetheless, it is true that Japan achieved significant economic recovery only after the outbreak of the Korean War. Japan's economic recovery was greatly accelerated by the wartime procurement of Japanese products and services by U.S. military forces. But it must be remembered that U.S. economic assistance before the Korean War had prepared the industrial basis for Japan to take advantage of the greatly expanded U.S. military procurement during that war.

*   *   *

In March 1947, General MacArthur expressed his desire that a formal peace agreement with Japan be made within one year. In response, the U.S. government proposed to the other member nations of the Far Eastern Commission that a preliminary peace conference be held. But the U.S. negotiations with those nations were soon stalled because of disagreement between the United States and two of its major former allies, the Soviet Union and China, over procedural matters. The United States decided to suspend negotiations, because its policymakers began to think that in view of the developing Cold War it would be better to give Japan more time for economic recovery and political stabilization before ending the occupation.

In 1949, however, a consensus emerged in the U.S. State Department that the occupation of Japan had now reached a stage of "diminishing returns." If the occupation were prolonged further, it would spoil the pro-American feelings that the benevolent occupation had succeeded in cultivating among the Japanese people. Secretary of State Dean Acheson felt that the United States should take the diplomatic initiative toward reaching an early peace settlement with Japan. However, his move to achieve an early peace settlement was blocked in the U.S. government by the Pentagon. Although General MacArthur in Tokyo wanted to end the occupation as soon as possible, military leaders in Washington were reluctant to part with the privilege of free, unrestricted use of Japanese military bases. President Truman favored the position of the State Department, but the military still hesitated.

The entrance of a new actor was necessary for the political scene in Washington to take a new turn. That new actor was John Foster Dulles. An influential Republican and an advocate of bipartisanship in foreign policy, Dulles was expected to handle the issue of peace with Japan without making it a partisan issue. He was well-known as an international law expert with considerable diplomatic experience. In addition, he had acquaintances in the Senate and the military. Because of these qualifications, in May 1950 the president entrusted Dulles with the task of moving forward the stalled policymaking process with regard to peace with Japan. At about that same time, in June, both a State Department mission headed by Dulles and a Pentagon mission that included Secretary of Defense Louis Johnson and the Joint Chiefs of Staff Chairman General Omar Bradley visited Tokyo for talks with MacArthur. Before the two U.S.

missions returned to Washington, they and MacArthur seemed to have reached a basic agreement. MacArthur, who had advocated an unarmed, neutral Japan, now agreed with the Pentagon leaders that a peace treaty should allow the United States to retain unrestricted use of military bases in Japan, and the Pentagon group was now inclined to accept the idea of an early peace treaty. In the same month, the Korean War broke out, and the United States decided to send armed forces to the Korean peninsula to defend the Republic of Korea. U.S. bases in Japan were indispensable for U.S. military action in Korea. But this did not stop the momentum in Washington for an early peace settlement with Japan. Early in September, the Joint Chiefs of Staff confirmed their willingness to accept both the principle of an early peace and the nature of the peace outlined by the State Department, on the condition that a treaty "should not come into effect until after favorable resolution of the military situation in Korea." Soon Dulles began preliminary discussions with Great Britain and other members of the Far Eastern Commission concerning the principles of a peace with Japan. A seven-point memorandum that outlined the U.S. plan for a formal peace with Japan was issued in November.

During the autumn of 1950, the United States was very optimistic about the Korean situation. However, toward the end of November, when massive Chinese ground forces began to enter the Korean Peninsula, the situation suddenly became very critical. In January 1951, the Korean War was in a very difficult phase for the United States, but President Truman decided not to delay a peace settlement with Japan. In a letter addressed to Dulles, the president stated: "The United States should proceed with further steps to bring about a peace settlement with Japan without awaiting a favorable resolution of the military situation in Korea." He explained the policy of the United States toward the Pacific region as follows: "The United States will commit substantial armed force to the defense of the island chain of which Japan forms a part"; "it desires that Japan should increasingly acquire the ability to defend itself"; "it is willing to make a mutual-assistance arrangement with the Pacific island nations," including Japan.

Dulles held a series of bilateral talks with the foreign ministers of the United States' major wartime allies and the Pacific nations so as to build an international consensus, with minimum revisions to satisfy other governments, regarding the U.S. plan for peace with Japan. For the United States, a peace settlement with Japan was not merely a peace settlement, but a means by which to make Japan an American ally. Thus, Dulles had a series of talks with Japanese Prime Minister Yoshida to obtain the latter's consent concerning the nature of the peace settlement envisaged by the United States. If Japan was willing to align itself with the United States, Japan could expect a generous peace arranged for by the United States.

When Dulles arrived in Tokyo in January 1951, he told the reporters that he regarded Japan not as a party to be dictated to, but as one to be consulted with. Yoshida was glad to align Japan with the United States so as to obtain military protection and economic assistance from the latter. But he resisted Dulles's request for Japanese rearmament. Because the rearmament of Japan as an American ally was the major aim of Dulles' mission, he wanted a concrete promise from the prime minister. Yoshida, understanding that he could not let Dulles leave Tokyo empty-handed, handed him a short memorandum that promised that when a peace treaty went into effect, Japan would create "security forces, land and sea, totaling 50,000," which would mark "the start of Japan's new democratic armed forces." This promise barely met Dulles's condition for a peace settlement. Yoshida insisted on keeping the promise secret, and Dulles agreed to this condition.

Yoshida wanted to have a U.S. commitment to defend Japan in return for the offer of the privilege to have military bases in Japan. But Dulles was not inclined to give a clear U.S. commitment concerning the defense of Japan until Japan became ready to develop military forces on a considerable scale. Japan's passive attitude regarding rearmament, together with negative responses of Britain and several Pacific countries to the idea of a Pacific pact, discouraged the United States from pursuing a Pacific version of NATO.

With regard to territorial matters, Yoshida tried to get U.S. recognition of Japan's sovereignty over the Ryukyu (Okinawa) and Bonin (Ogasawara) Islands, but his efforts were frustrated. Dulles, prior to his visit to Japan, for a while thought of recognizing Japan's sovereignty over these islands under certain conditions, but he gave up the idea because of strong objections from the U.S. military. It was very unfortunate that Okinawa was destined to be left out of the peace settlement. The profound effect of that is still felt in Okinawa.

Thus, there were issues concerning which Yoshida did not obtain a favorable response from Dulles. But the peace agreement that the United States was trying to bring forth was on the whole a generous one for a defeated nation. The United States wanted a peace that would not burden Japan with any obligation of reparation payments, and it did not want to limit Japan's economic or military capabilities. Also, the United States did not plan to establish an international commission to oversee Japan's compliance with the peace treaty. Although in the process of negotiations the United States yielded to the strong demands of several Asian countries for reparations, the treaty limited Japan's reparations to offering Japanese products and services. Except for this minor concession, the United States succeeded in bringing forth the peace settlement it had envisaged in 1950. Britain and several Commonwealth nations wanted to limit Japan's economic capabilities because of their fear of its revival as a formidable industrial power, but Dulles persuaded them to agree with the U.S. position on that issue.

Given that the world was divided by the Cold War, and given that a hot war was still taking place in Korea, a peace settlement between Japan and all the wartime Allied countries seemed to be difficult to achieve. The Soviet Union, known to be very critical of the nature of the peace settlement designed by the United States, was expected to boycott the peace conference. No government from China—neither the Communist government of the People's Republic nor the Nationalist Chinese government in exile in Taiwan —was invited, because the two cosponsors of the peace conference, the United States and Great Britain, could not agree as to which government should be invited. They agreed that after Japan regained its sovereign status it should choose one of the two Chinese governments as the representative of that country and make peace with it. The Allied–Japan peace conference was held in San Francisco in September 1951. The Soviet Union and several Soviet-bloc countries sent delegations to San Francisco and tried to propose motions to revise the treaty being presented to the conference. But because it was the intention of the United States government to make the conference a ceremonial occasion at which each delegation would sign the peace treaty that had already been agreed upon by many former Allied Powers, the American host of the conference blocked every Soviet attempt to present a motion. The San Francisco Peace Treaty was signed on September 8 by the envoys of 49 nations. On the same day, the Japan–U.S. Security Treaty was signed.

The San Francisco peace settlement was a diplomatic success for the United States in several respects. First, the United States gave Japan generous peace conditions that would facilitate the latter's economic recovery and enable it to grow as America's reliable partner in Asia. Second, the United States was able to retain military bases in Japan and to continue the military control of strategically important Okinawa. Third, the United States imposed upon Japan a moral obligation to develop self-defense capability as an American ally. Fourth, the United States successfully excluded the Soviet Union and the People's Republic of China from the peace settlement, and later let Japan establish diplomatic relations with Nationalist China.

Part of the Japanese public was opposed to the peace settlement, which lacked the participation of the two Communist giants, the Soviet Union and the People's Republic of China, and which, through the security treaty with the United States, aligned Japan with one camp of the Cold War rivals. But a majority of the Japanese people wanted a U.S. military presence, at least for the time being, to ensure Japan's security. Although they were not satisfied with all the articles of the San Francisco treaties, they welcomed the opportunity for Japan to regain its sovereignty, and they favored the ratification of the two treaties.

2. JAPAN'S DESIRE FOR A MORE INDEPENDENT DIPLOMACY AND A GREATER VOICE IN THE SECURITY ARRANGEMENT

Prime Minister Yoshida thought that Japan should regain a viable national economy before developing its armed forces. His policy therefore gave priority to economic recovery while limiting rearmament efforts to the minimum. For the time being, he thought, Japan should depend for its security on the military presence of the United States in Asia. This policy orientation, which political scientists later referred to as the Yoshida Doctrine, was challenged on the left by the opponents of the security arrangement with the United States and on the right by the advocates of genuine rearmament through constitutional revision. Both of them were not satisfied with the existing security treaty with the United States. The U.S. government was not satisfied with Yoshida's stance on the issue of rearmament, either.

The United States suggested that Japan speed up its rearmament by making use of the Mutual Security Assistance (MSA) program, and American officials exhorted the Japanese government to make greater rearmament efforts. Yoshida was interested in the MSA program, in part because he thought it was time to create Japanese armed forces on a small scale, and in part because he expected that MSA aid could be used to help Japan's economic recovery. Although negotiations for a mutual security assistance agreement began in 1953, it took much time for the two governments to agree on the size of the projected Japanese ground force. Japan planned a gradual increase of the size of its ground forces from 110,000 to 180,000 personnel, but the United States wanted Japan to develop its army to a total of 300,000. In the end, the United States accepted Japan's number only as the initial step to be achieved within two years.

The two governments signed an MSA agreement in March 1954, and the Yoshida cabinet introduced two defense bills before the Diet. When these bills became law in June 1950, the Defense Agency was created, and the Security Forces were reorganized as the Self-Defense Forces, composed of ground, maritime, and air forces. Japan thus came to possess, in spite of Article 9 of the Constitution of 1946, what can be regarded as genuine armed forces, however small in size.

❊   ❊   ❊

While the Japanese government was trying to push the defense bills through a stormy Diet session in the spring of 1954, there took place an unfortunate incident that rocked Japan–U.S. relations. In March 1954, a Japanese fishing-vessel named *Fukuryū*

Maru No. 5 was showered by radioactive ashes from a hydrogen-bomb test explosion. The ship was about 65 miles east of Bikini, the test site, and was 14 miles outside of the designated off-limits zone. The crew of the vessel became sick and were hospitalized upon returning to Japan. One of them died six months later. And because the tuna-fish catch of the *Fukuryū Maru* indicated a high level of radioactive contamination, there was a panic in the Japanese fish market. All fish caught in the central Pacific were examined for radioactive contamination, and a large quantity of fish was abandoned.

This incident caused quite an uproar in Japan, particularly because American officials were slow in expressing an apology. In Washington, American officials at first suspected that the vessel had been inside the designated off-limits zone, but the U.S. government later informed Tokyo that the designated zone was to be enlarged six times. Three weeks after the incident was known, Ambassador John M. Allison conveyed the American government's first expression of deep regret for the incident and confirmed that just compensation would be paid to the victims. But much resentment had already arisen in Japan.

The people of Japan, as the nation that had experienced atomic bombing of its cities of Hiroshima and Nagasaki, were already especially sensitive to nuclear weapons and nuclear tests. The *Fukuryū Maru* incident stimulated a mass movement to prohibit atomic and hydrogen bombs and nuclear-test explosions. Because of this sensitivity, the incident led to the emergence of anti-American feelings among grassroots Japanese people. As a result, neutralism seemed to be gaining influence among the people of Japan. This was the first crisis in postwar Japan–U.S. relations, and it revealed a wide gap between the requirements of the American global strategy and the Japanese antinuclear sentiment that resulted from America's use of atomic bombs against Hiroshima and Nagasaki.

Ambassador Allison felt that the neutralist influence in Japan should not be underestimated. He believed that excessive American pressure on Japan for a speedy military buildup might drive Japan towards neutralism. In September 1954, he advised the U.S. government that it would be better for the United States to reconsider priorities regarding its Japan policies, because the basic long-term interests of the United States would best be served by the development of Japan as a partner with a stable government, a viable economy, and prestige in the international community.

The policymakers in Washington took note of Allison's advice. The National Security Council stated, in a policy paper (NSC 5516/1) adopted in April 1955, "The United States should avoid pressing the Japanese to increase their military forces to the prejudice of political and economic stability." In the second half of the 1950s, the United States eased its pressure on Japan for a military buildup.

It should be remembered that international tensions in Asia seemed to be reduced to some degree in 1954, as the Indochina armistice followed the Korean armistice that had been agreed upon in the previous year. The Indochina armistice was agreed upon at the Geneva Conference, which was participated in by all of the major powers in both camps of the Cold War, including the People's Republic of China. The new Communist leadership in post-Stalin Russia was emphasizing the possibility of "peaceful coexistence" between the two Cold War camps. Thus, there was an international trend that might encourage Japanese neutralism. Reflecting strong Japanese interest in trade with China, the Yoshida Cabinet had adopted the principle of "separation of economic relations from political relations." As early as June 1952, a group of politicians had privately visited Beijing and entered into an unofficial Sino–Japanese trade agreement. Soon after the end of the Korean War, the Japanese Diet adopted a Sino-Japanese trade-promotion resolution that required Japan's government to remove special restrictions imposed upon that country's trade with mainland China. In Washington, President Dwight D. Eisenhower took an understanding attitude toward Japan's need for trade relations with China. But other officials entertained more-negative views on that issue, expressing their fear that if Sino–Japanese trade developed, the Japanese might tilt toward neutralism. Dulles accordingly warned the Japanese government against going too far in developing trade relations with Communist China.

*   *   *

In 1954, Prime Minister Yoshida, who had been in office since 1948, fell out of favor with the Japanese people. The *Fukuryū Maru* incident helped to weaken popular support for Yoshida, because many Japanese felt that he was excessively subservient to the United States. But the primary cause of popular discontent against him was his handling of a ship-building scandal. By the time he left for a trip to America and Europe late in September of 1954, his opponents both inside and outside his Liberal Party were working vigorously for the overthrow of his cabinet. Yoshida was forced to resign early in December, and Ichirō Hatoyama, the leader of the anti-Yoshida conservatives, became his successor. Hatoyama was a conservative nationalist. He stood for revising Article 9 of the Constitution so as to permit the development of normal military forces, and he also wanted to make the Japan–U.S. security arrangement a more-equal and more-reciprocal one. However, Hatoyama also was a proponent of independent diplomacy and of more normal relations with Japan's Communist neighbors.

In the general election of February 1955, Hatoyama's Democratic Party increased its seats in the lower house at the expense of the Liberals. But his party remained a minority in that house. This lack of majority support in the Diet and the prospect of the birth of a united socialist party stimulated a merger movement among members of the two conservative parties. In the fall of 1955, these two parties merged as the Liberal Democratic Party (LDP). At about that same time, two socialist parties united as the Socialist Party. The Socialist Party would always be strong enough to prevent the LDP from revising the constitution. But the Socialists were never able to end the LDP's majority in the Diet, allowing the latter's perennial rule. Thus the two-party system created in 1955 was an extraordinary one, consisting of two parties of quite unequal strength.

The Soviet Union noticed Hatoyama's interest in improving Japan's relations with it. When the Soviet Union conveyed to Japan its willingness to begin negotiations toward a peace treaty, Hatoyama responded with enthusiasm. Because the United States retained diplomatic relations with the Soviet Union, it was quite reasonable for Japan to hope to establish diplomatic relations with that Communist giant. But the U.S. government was afraid that if Japan succeeded in establishing diplomatic relations with the Soviet Union, it might then be tempted also to have diplomatic relations with the People's Republic of China. The United States was concerned that Japan's opening of diplomatic relations with the Soviet Union might trigger Japan's drift toward a neutralist position. The United States therefore always advised Japan to be cautious in its approach to the Soviet Union, and it warned Japan against making easy concessions to that country concerning the territorial issue. U.S. support of Japan's territorial claims to Etorofu and Kunashiri had the effect of encouraging hard-liners within the LDP and therefore of hardening Japan's negotiating stance vis-à-vis the Soviet Union. Negotiations were deadlocked because the two nations could not agree on territorial matters. Finally, Hatoyama decided to open Japan's diplomatic relations with the Soviet Union through a joint declaration without agreement on territorial issues. He thus achieved his purpose of establishing formal relations between the two countries. This, in turn, opened the way for Japan to be admitted to the United Nations in December 1956.

When Hatoyama retired after these diplomatic achievements, Tanzan Ishibashi was elected as his successor in December 1956. Ishibashi, too, advocated improvement of Japan's relations with its Communist neighbors and hoped to develop economic and political relations with the People's Republic of China. But he had to resign in March 1957 because of an illness. The post of the prime minister went to his Vice-Prime Minister Nobusuke Kishi.

＊　＊　＊

Nobusuke Kishi, who had been held in the Sugamo Prison after World War II as a war criminal for having served as a minister in General Hideki Tojō's wartime cabinet, made a phenomenal comeback to become an important political figure in postwar Japan. He was a nationalist, but he was acutely aware of American power. He favored a firm partnership with the United States, which he believed would enable Japan to play the role of a major power in Asia. He was not very interested in improving Japan's relations

with its Communist neighbors. Because of his policy outlook, the
United States showed a much higher regard for Kishi than it had
shown for his two predecessors. "Mr. Kishi gives every indication
of being the strongest government leader to emerge in postwar
Japan," Dulles wrote in a memorandum to Eisenhower. "With his
coming to power," Dulles believed, "a period of drift" in Japan
was over. The United States welcomed Kishi warmly and gave him
wide publicity during his visit in June 1957.

It was Kishi's desire to put Japan–U.S. relations on a more-equal
basis by revising the terms of the two nations' security treaty.
Remembering, however, Dulles' cold response to Foreign Minister
Mamoru Shigemitsu's plea in 1955 to revise that treaty, Kishi
approached this issue cautiously. Dulles now took a more positive
attitude toward the issue of revision of the security treaty, because
he considered it important for the United States to work with Kishi
for greater mutuality in the Japan–U.S. security relationship. A
Kishi–Eisenhower joint statement announced their agreement to set
up a joint committee to discuss how to adjust the security arrangements. But this committee did not actually take up the issue of
revision of the security treaty, but limited its discussion to adjustment within the terms of the existing treaty. Officials of the
Japanese Foreign Ministry thought that it was not possible to conclude a new treaty of mutual defense with United States without
revising Japan's constitution. They were therefore thinking only of
supplementing the existing treaty with some declarations.

It was Ambassador Douglas MacArthur II, a nephew and
namesake of the famous supreme commander, who conceived a
prototype of a new security treaty and impressed the United
States about the merits of concluding such a treaty with Japan—a
treaty that did not impose any military obligations upon Japan
outside its own territories, while requiring the United States to
defend Japan. MacArthur understood that Kishi wanted a new
security treaty, and he, too, believed that a new treaty would better satisfy the Japanese national sentiment and would establish
the Japan–U.S. relationship on a firmer basis. When in August
1958 MacArthur asked Kishi about the latter's preference, Kishi
of course said that he preferred a new treaty to partial revision of
the existing one. In September, Foreign Minister Aiichirō

Fujiyama visited Washington to confer with Secretary of State Dulles. Dulles told Fujiyama that because he considered the spirit of friendship to be much more important than legal privileges and obligations, he was willing to negotiate a new treaty that might require the United States to concede much for little gain. However, Dulles did not live to sign the new security treaty. Because of a serious illness, he resigned as secretary of state on April 15, 1959, and died the following month.

Kishi and Fujiyama wanted the new treaty to embody such points as: (1) the United States should assume an obligation to help Japan defend itself against external attack; (2) Japan's obligations should be limited to those compatible with its constitution; (3) the treaty should be effective for a limited period; (4) the United States should consult with Japan before changing the disposition and/or equipment of U.S. forces in Japan or using bases in Japan for operational purposes to ensure peace and security in the Far East. Ambassador MacArthur prepared a draft treaty that satisfied Japanese points (1), (2), and (3), and a draft declaration that satisfied point (4); negotiations began in Tokyo on the basis of those American drafts. The Japanese negotiators wanted two revisions to the draft treaty: (1) the term "collective defense" should be deleted from the text; and (2) the treaty area should not be extended to include the Pacific region. Although this treaty did not require Japan to send armed forces outside Japan, the initial U.S. proposal to extend the treaty area was too drastic for Japan. MacArthur soon understood that it was politically infeasible for the Japanese government to agree to the American draft on those points. When the Americans accepted these revisions, the American draft was satisfactory to the Japanese. If there had been no internal problem in Japan, the new treaty might have been signed even before the end of 1958. But there arose a problem in Japan, though not an anti-treaty movement led by opposition parties, but disunity within Kishi's own political party, the LDP.

At that time, the Liberal Democratic Party was a coalition of several factions of conservative politicians, just as it is today. Kishi had tried to weaken the factions that were unfriendly to his position, so as to consolidate his power, but that move was counterproductive. Some faction leaders became more unwilling to cooperate in supporting controversial legislation in the Diet. Their refusal to support a police-practices bill in December 1958 was a case in point. With his party in disarray, Kishi had to give up that controversial bill, which was much opposed by the Socialists and by labor organizations. It was Kishi's tactical mistake to take up a minor, but politically charged, issue when he should have concentrated his efforts on revision of the security treaty. Because of this domestic political crisis, Kishi had to ask Ambassador MacArthur to suspend the treaty-revision negotiations for a while. It took several months for Kishi to restore order in the LDP and to obtain the party's formal support of a new security treaty as outlined by his foreign minister. The party's faction chiefs gave Kishi formal support of his efforts to revise the treaty, but on the condition that the government should simultaneously negotiate with the United States for substantial revision of the executive agreement. That was exactly what both Kishi and MacArthur had wanted to do after the signing of a new treaty, because that had been expected to be very time-consuming. The rivals of Kishi and Fujiyama within the LDP, unwilling to allow those two leaders to get credit for what now seemed to be an easy task, burdened them with a new task. Some of them feared that Fujiyama, a wealthy newcomer, might later claim party leadership on the basis of his diplomatic success.

The negotiators for the two governments resumed their meetings in late April of 1959 and continued to meet regularly until January 1960, when the treaty, together with the executive agreement and other documents, were signed in Washington. But most of these meetings were devoted to negotiations for a new executive agreement that should be effective simultaneously with the treaty itself.

The new security treaty had greater mutuality than the one it replaced. For instance, in Article IV it stipulated, "The Parties will consult together from time to time regarding the implementation of this Treaty, and, at the request of either Party, whenever the security of Japan or international peace and security in the Far East is threatened." But mutuality in Article V was rather in form, than in substance. It read: "Each Party recognizes that an armed attack against either Party in the territories under the administration of

Japan would be dangerous to its own peace and security and declares that it would act to meet the common danger in accordance with its constitutional provisions and process." This meant that while the United States assumed an obligation to defend Japan if Japan were attacked, Japan was obligated to defend against external attack only the military bases in Japan that had been offered to the United States to use to ensure the security of Japan and international peace and security in the Far East. In a supplemental document, the two parties agreed that "Major changes in the deployment into Japan of United States armed forces, major changes in their equipment, and the use of facilities and areas in Japan as bases for military combat operations to be undertaken from Japan other than those conducted under Article V of the said Treaty, shall be the subject of prior consultation with the Government of Japan."

Japanese critics of the new security treaty argued that its greater mutuality meant that Japan would be implicated more deeply with the Cold War military strategy of the United States, while throwing doubt on the effectiveness of the stipulation of "prior consultation" in restraining U.S. action. The leftist opposition groups, much encouraged by disharmony within the LDP, which had given them a taste of victory in the dispute over the police-practices bill, decided to organize a movement to prevent the ratification of the revised security treaty. But opposition leaders themselves did not expect that they would succeed in cornering Kishi with a massive protest movement. However, some international incidents, such as the U-2 affair and the subsequent cancellation of the Paris summit, further stimulated the anti-treaty movement. But the direct cause of the political turmoil in May and June of 1960 was Kishi's decision to push the treaty through the lower house by devious means so that the treaty could be ratified by the time of President Eisenhower's visit to Tokyo in June of that year. If Kishi had called for a general election in the spring, he would have succeeded more easily in securing the approval of the lower house for the new treaty without much public criticism. However, he again made a tactical mistake. Opposition to the treaty was now joined by opposition to Kishi's open disregard of the spirit of parliamentary democracy. Anti-government demonstrations again took place in

Tokyo, and they spread to cities in various prefectures across the nation.

Informed of the political turmoil in Japan, Eisenhower and Secretary of State Christian Herter considered postponing their visit for about two months. In Tokyo, Ambassador MacArthur told a Foreign Ministry official that he thought postponement was advisable. But Kishi strongly desired to have the presidential visit in June as scheduled. Opponents of Kishi and his security treaty were now strongly against the visit of the president because they feared Kishi would make use of the presidential visit to escape from the current political crisis. It was very unfortunate that the issue of the presidential visit was entangled with the intensified political struggle between the Kishi government and his opponents in Japan. When Eisenhower's press secretary James Hagerty arrived in Tokyo to arrange the detailed schedule of the presidential visit, the car in which he was riding with Ambassador MacArthur was surrounded near the airport by demonstrators shouting their opposition to the planned visit of the president to Japan. The two Americans had to be rescued by helicopter. In Washington, Herter felt that the incident had caused "grave misgivings" among those who had staunchly supported the visit. However, because the Japanese government still hoped to have Eisenhower visit as scheduled, the president and his party left Washington for a tour in East Asia. Only at the last moment, when Eisenhower was in Manila, did the Kishi cabinet decide to ask the president to postpone his visit to Japan. Kishi resigned after the treaty went into effect. In July of 1960, Hayato Ikeda was elected as Kishi's successor. After Kishi's resignation, the anti-government mass movement subsided, and in the general election in November the LDP gained a handsome majority in the lower house.

The episode of 1960 belonged to an era in which Japan retained a small-nation inferiority complex while America considered itself the protector of the free world. A small-nation complex underlay both Kishi's desire to replace the old security treaty with a new one and the anti-treaty fever, which was a form of national self-assertiveness. Most participants in demonstrations were certainly anti-Kishi, but were much less anti-American. And America, because of its protector mentality, did not want to retaliate against the Japanese for the Hagerty incident and the cancellation of Eisenhower's visit. The cooperative relationship between Japan and the United States, though disrupted in the turmoil of May–June 1960, was able to restart under new leaders on both sides on the basis of the new security treaty.

3. TOWARD A MORE EQUAL PARTNERSHIP

The primary item on Prime Minister Hayato Ikeda's agenda was to restore Japan's political stability by regaining the people's confidence in the LDP government. For this purpose, he coined the attractive catch-phrase "income doubling" and promised to double the national income within 10 years. Ikeda concentrated his efforts on promoting economic growth and avoided raising divisive constitutional or foreign-policy issues.

Ikeda believed that a prosperous Japan would be able both to maintain political and social stability at home and to contribute to political stability and economic development in Asia. That was the role he envisaged for Japan as an ally of the United States. Because Japan's economic prosperity depended much on amicable relations with the United States, it was the urgent task of Ikeda's diplomacy to repair Japan–U.S. relations, which had been disrupted by the political turmoil of the spring of 1960 and particularly by Tokyo's request that President Eisenhower's visit to Japan be postponed.

America's new president, John F. Kennedy, also believed that it was important to repair Japan–U.S. relations. He pleased the Japanese by choosing as the American ambassador to Japan Professor Edwin O. Reischauer, the foremost American Japanologist, who was already well-known in Japan. When Ikeda visited Washington in June 1961, Kennedy proposed to strengthen the Japan–U.S. partnership by creating a joint committee on trade and economy, to be composed of cabinet members of the two nations. Ikeda was delighted, because trade and economy were the areas in which he especially wanted to develop Japan's close relations with the United States. Later, another joint committee was organized to develop cooperative relations in the fields of culture, education, and science. Thus, opportunities for bilateral dialogue were developed in the 1960s, contributing to mutual understanding between Japan and the United States. As a result, both sides better understood which interests and views they shared and which ones they did not share.

Meanwhile, Ambassador Reischauer was working energetically to develop a dialogue with the Japanese people. It was he who had commented in 1960 that it had been the lack of a U.S. dialogue with the Japanese people that had caused the disruption in Japan–U.S. relations. During his tenure, Reischauer not only invited a variety of people to his residence, but he also visited many places to meet many people, gave public lectures, and participated in forums. Because a sizable portion of Japanese intellectuals and students were leaning toward the left politically and were critical of American policy in Asia, he took special care to visit universities so as to meet academics and students. Through these exchanges, he contributed much to the growth of an amicable relationship between the two nations. No other ambassador has made as great an effort as he did in reaching out to the Japanese people.

Ikeda, because of his keen interest in expanding Japan's trade, visited Britain and the EEC countries to develop Japan's economic ties with Western Europe. In London, Ikeda was able to sign a new Anglo–Japanese commercial treaty by which Britain withdrew its application of GATT Article XXXV to Japanese trade. Very soon thereafter, other Western European countries followed Britain in removing obstacles to Japanese trade. Ikeda was very much impressed by the economic resurgence of Western Europe, and he felt that if Japan developed its economy further, economic strength would become Japan's great diplomatic asset. Thus, his diplomacy aimed to make Japan an acknowledged member of the international community of advanced nations. His aim was achieved in 1964, when Japan became an Article-8 country of the International Monetary Fund (IMF) and a member of the Organization for Economic Cooperation and Development (OECD).

Ikeda was also interested in developing trade with Japan's big neighbor, the People's Republic of China. That nation had suspended trade with Japan in 1958, but it was highly desirable for the People's Republic, whose alliance with the Soviet Union was much strained, to resume trade with Japan. As a result, Japan and China allowed their respective semiofficial agents to conclude a trade agreement in October 1962. Ikeda knew well the United States' view on this issue, for it had advised Japan against developing trade with mainland China. But Ikeda went forward on this issue, believing that developing trade relations would encourage China to take a friendly posture toward Japan. But the U.S. view of China was quite different. When the Joint Committee on Trade and Economy met in Washington in the following month, President Kennedy emphasized the danger that Communist China might try to dominate all of Asia, and he expressed his hope that Japan as an American ally would seriously consider what Japan could do to meet this danger. Because the Nationalist Chinese regime in Taipei reacted strongly against the development of trade relations between Japan and Communist China, and because the United States expressed its concern about the deterioration of the Japan–Taiwan relationship, the Ikeda cabinet had to do its best to soothe Taiwan's wounded feelings, but this effort in turn displeased mainland China. Thus, it was very difficult for Japan to keep a proper balance between Beijing and Taipei.

Although most Japanese did not share Kennedy's strong anti-Chinese view, they welcomed Kennedy's détente with Khrushchev in 1963. The Japanese media were very friendly toward Kennedy during his tenure. He was by far the most popular American president in postwar Japan. His assassination was a great shock to the Japanese people.

In 1964, Ikeda was suffering from cancer, but he remained in office until after the Tokyo Olympic Games. After that great sports festival was successfully closed for the host nation, Eisaku Satō succeeded Ikeda as prime minister. Unlike Ikeda, who tended to limit his diplomatic efforts to the economic aspect of international relations, Satō was willing to tackle issues of a more political nature, such as establishing diplomatic relations with the Republic of Korea, which was objected to by parties on the left in Japan. In June 1965, Japan and South Korea signed a treaty to establish diplomatic relations. In August, Satō visited Okinawa, the first time for a postwar Japanese prime minister to do so. While there, he made his famous statement that until Okinawa was returned to Japan, the postwar era would not end for Japan. Thus he elevated the reversion of Okinawa to the top of his diplomatic agenda.

When Satō took up the Okinawa problem in his first meeting with President Lyndon B. Johnson in January 1965, the latter had stated only that he "looks forward to the day when the security interests of the free world in the Far East will permit" the return of the administrative control of the islands to Japan. As a result, Satō's sudden announcement of his determination regarding that issue stunned Foreign Ministry officials. That did not seem to be an opportune time to raise the reversion issue, because the United States had just started to expand its military action in Vietnam. Because U.S. bases in Okinawa were important as support bases for U.S. military activities, Washington would be more reluctant than before to part with the military administration of Okinawa. Some critics predicted that this might lead to Satō's downfall.

But the timing of his announcement actually was not so bad. There was growing awareness within the U.S. government that if people in Okinawa became exceedingly hostile toward the United States, it would be impossible for the United States to maintain military bases there. What is more, resentment against the United States might spread among Japanese on the main islands, weakening their support of the Japan–U.S. alliance. As a result, U.S. officials began to ponder what policy would best enable the United States to maintain its military bases in strategic Okinawa for a long period. Satō's statement therefore became a factor in activating Washington's policy-reviewing process. When Satō visited Washington in November 1967, President Johnson displayed an understanding attitude toward Satō's desire that Tokyo and Washington should agree within a few years on a date for the return of Okinawa, and he agreed with Satō that the two governments should begin joint examination of the status of Okinawa. But the Johnson administration, preoccupied with the serious military situation in Vietnam, did not have time in 1968 to give much attention to the Okinawa problem. But the United States returned the Bonin Islands (Ogasawara) to Japan in June of that year.

President Johnson had achieved significant reforms in welfare and civil rights, but the outburst of racial riots in many cities and Johnson's fruitless escalation of military action in Vietnam had alienated many voters from his administration and the Democratic Party. In the presidential election of 1968, in which Johnson did not run, Richard M. Nixon, the Republican candidate, was elected. It was during the Nixon era that Okinawa was returned to Japan. President Nixon and his advisor Henry A. Kissinger favored returning the administration of Okinawa to Japan without delay.

The most delicate problem relating to the return of Okinawa was whether the United States was willing to accept the application of the same restrictions on the use of military bases in Okinawa as were applied to the use of those elsewhere in Japan. Public opinion in both Japan and Okinawa strongly demanded that the bases in Okinawa should be subject to the same conditions as other bases in Japan, that is, subject to the principles of "prior consultation" and "no nuclear weapons." Prime Minister Satō feared that unless those conditions were accepted by the United States, his efforts for the return of Okinawa would not be much appreciated by the public in Japan, particularly in Okinawa. Thus, he tried to obtain Nixon's consent to these two conditions. Nixon was willing to agree, but wanted the United States to have the right to reintroduce nuclear weapons to Okinawa in an emergency.

When Satō visited Washington in 1969 to meet President Nixon, the two leaders agreed that the reversion should take place in 1972. As for the removal of nuclear weapons, the joint Satō–Nixon declaration stated that "that without prejudice to the position of the United States Government with respect to the prior consultation system . . . the reversion would be carried out in a manner consistent with the policy of the Japanese government as described by the Prime Minister." This sentence hinted that the United States might request the consent of the Japanese government to reintroduce nuclear weapons to Okinawa in emergency cases. It is now believed, as a scholar very close to the prime minister wrote in his book a few years ago, that Satō then signed a secret memorandum to assure Nixon that such a request would promptly be accepted by the Japanese government.

Although the existence of that memorandum was unknown at that time, there was considerable criticism of this part of the joint declaration in Japan. Japanese opposition parties were also critical of Satō's acknowledgment that the security of the Republic of Korea and the peace and security of the Taiwan area were very important for Japan's own security. Nevertheless, Satō's approach to the Okinawa reversion gained wide public support because of Nixon's acceptance of the two conditions concerning the use of military bases in Okinawa.

In June 1971, the two governments signed the Okinawa Reversion Agreement. Chōbyō Yara, the chief executive of the Ryukyu government, in his statement expressed gratitude for the efforts of the Japanese government in bringing forth this great historic moment, but he could not but regret that the wish of the Okinawans for a substantial reduction of the number of U.S. bases was not yet fulfilled. Given the high concentration of U.S. bases in Okinawa, he maintained, the so-called principle that the bases in Okinawa should be subject to the same conditions as other bases in Japan was simply unreal. The agreement was approved by the National Diet in December 1971, and the reversion took place in May 1972. The United States relinquished control over Okinawa, which had continued for 27 years since 1945, thus removing that thorny issue in Japan–U.S. relations. But that did not mean that the Okinawa question was entirely resolved. Because the Okinawan people continue to resent the high concentration of U.S. bases in their prefecture, a situation that has not changed much since the day of the reversion, Japan and the United States still have to tackle the difficult task of how to satisfy both the security requirements and the desire of the Okinawans.

Satō was Japan's prime minister for seven and one-half years, from November 1964 to July 1972—the longest term for a Japanese prime minister since World War II. His tenure largely corresponded with the Vietnam War era. As the leader of an American ally in Asia, an important problem for his foreign policy was how to cope with the Vietnam War.

Asian allies of the United States, most notably the Republic of Korea and Australia, sent armed forces to Vietnam. Japan was the only country among American allies in Asia that did not do so. Although President Johnson desired at least the token presence of Japanese Self-Defense Forces in Vietnam, Prime Minister Satō had no intention to comply, for both political as well as constitutional reasons. He strictly limited Japan's support of South Vietnam to sending medical and other supplies for Vietnamese civilians. But in his public statements, Satō always endorsed the American war aims in Vietnam. To compensate for its negative attitude to military cooperation in Vietnam, Satō's government tried to impress the United States with Japan's active contributions toward nonmilitary, particularly economic, cooperation among noncommunist countries in Asia.

It should also be noted that Japan significantly helped America's war efforts in Vietnam in passive and indirect ways, inasmuch as U.S. air and naval bases in Japan, as well as those in Okinawa, served as support bases for U.S. military actions in Vietnam. Also, U.S. warships and military planes used Japanese bases to be repaired and to get new supplies, and U.S. military personnel came to Japan for rest or medical treatment. As one American high-ranking naval officer stated, it would have been impossible for America to fight the war in Vietnam without bases in Japan and Okinawa. In this sense, Japan served well as an American ally.

During the Vietnam War, the U.S. military bought a considerable amount of goods and services in Japan. Japanese profited from these U.S. military purchases and profits from these sources helped Japan's phenomenal economic growth in the 1960s, though not as significantly as during the Korean War. Some Americans therefore felt that while they were fighting a fierce war in Vietnam, the Japanese were only making money. But as the Vietnam War became increasingly unpopular in America, so did it in Japan. Stimulated by the rise of antiwar activism in America, an anti-Vietnam War movement became active in Japan. Because the Japanese TV media were broadcasting the same war scenes that appeared in the American media, the Japanese public became increasingly critical of America's war in Vietnam. In Japanese public-opinion polls, the percentage of those who rated the United States as the most likable nation dropped sharply during those years. In addition, because scenes of racial riots in American cities were also televised in Japan, the sweet image of the United States that the Japanese people had held began to weaken. In spite of the pro-American stance of the Satō government, there was a gap between the stance of the government and that of the media and the vocal public. Thus, the escalation of the Vietnam War tended to strain Japanese–American relations.

4. CONFLICT AND COOPERATION IN AN AGE OF JAPAN'S ECONOMIC ASCENDANCY

Before the Okinawa reversion took place, Japan and the United States experienced a textile wrangle, the worst trade dispute in Japan–U.S. relations. In the presidential election of 1968, the Republican candidate Nixon needed the votes of Southern states to win. He therefore promised to defend the interests of the Southern textile industry and its workers by reducing the volume of textile imports from Asia. Soon after his inauguration, Nixon ordered the Commerce Department to open negotiations with the Japanese government regarding the reduction of Japanese textile exports to the United States, wanting Japan to voluntarily adopt a quota for textile exports to the United States. But the U.S. demand met strong resistance in Japan. Not only the Japanese textile industry but also the Ministry of International Trade and Industry (MITI) was opposed to a voluntary export quota. Diet members were also sympathetic to Japan's textile interests. Japan's Minister of International Trade and Industry Masayoshi Ōhira argued that there should be no voluntary export restriction unless there was clear evidence that Japanese exports had injured the American textile industry.

When Prime Minister Satō visited Washington in November 1969, President Nixon raised the textile-quota issue, indicating his personal political interest in this issue. Satō seemed to understand the importance of this issue for Nixon and promised to take care of the problem. However, because there was strong opposition in Japan, Satō could not carry out his promise immediately. In October 1970, when Satō again saw Nixon in Washington, he again promised prompt action, but negotiations did not produce a quick result. In March 1971, the leaders of the

Japanese Textile Federation, who began to think that some kind of quota was unavoidable, contacted Congressman Wilbur Mills, the chairman of the U.S. House of Representative's powerful Ways and Means Committee, and obtained his endorsement of a relatively mild voluntary export quota. When the federation announced this voluntary quota, the spokesman of the Japanese government endorsed it and carelessly declared that intergovernmental negotiations on this issue would no longer be necessary, thereby revealing Tokyo's insensitivity to the delicate relationship that existed between President Nixon and Congressman Mills. Nixon reacted sharply against this statement by the Japanese government. Nixon rejected the quota plan as insufficient and criticized the attitude of the Japanese government in regarding the dispute as settled. If Japan was unwilling to resume government-to-government negotiations and to produce a reasonable quota plan, he hinted threateningly, the United States would be forced to take unilateral measures to defend the interests of the American textile industry and its workers. From Nixon's viewpoint, Satō had betrayed his trust. Nixon was delivering to Satō that which Satō coveted, Okinawa, but Satō repeatedly failed to keep his promise to deliver what Nixon wanted most. What is more, Satō's government now stated that this problem had been settled by an agreement between the Japanese textile industry and Congressman Mills. It was as if Satō had thrown mud in Nixon's face. Nixon would never allow Mills to take a political prize from him. Nixon strongly believed that he himself should deliver to the Southerners that which he had promised. It is generally believed that Nixon's anger at Satō was one reason why he did not tell the Japanese government about Kissinger's diplomatic breakthrough with Beijing before that was publicly announced. It was only after Nixon's angry remarks that Satō appointed the energetic Kakuei Tanaka as minister of international trade and industry and instructed him to settle the dispute quickly. Tanaka was able to persuade the Japanese textile industry to accept a more-stringent quota with a promise of handsome compensation subsidies. As it turned out, however, the Japanese textile industry declined rapidly during the 1970s, failing even to fill the quota that its representatives had regarded as too low.

The textile dispute was a conflict between two declining industries that retained strong political influence in their respective countries. Trade disputes recurred between Japan and the United States through the 1970s, but the lesson of the textile case made the two governments handle them more skillfully.

For Satō and the Japanese, 1971 was the year of "Nixon shocks." If Nixon's angry reaction at Satō's mishandling of the textile dispute was the first shock, they should have expected the second and third that followed. Nixon and Kissinger were trying, through U.S.–Soviet détente and U.S.–Sino rapprochement, to reorient American foreign policy from the bipolar Cold War system to a U.S.-centered multipolar system. Kissinger's secret visit to Beijing in July 1971 was the first important step in their new diplomatic strategy. The sudden announcement by the White House that, as a result of Kissinger's talks with China's leaders, Nixon would visit that country in 1972 was a great surprise for the world, especially for Japan and America's other Asian allies. Former Ambassador Kōichirō Asakai had once said that his worst nightmare as Japan's ambassador to the United States was to wake up one morning to hear the news that the United States had opened diplomatic relations with the People's Republic of China. Something like his nightmare now came true. This sudden announcement of Nixon's intention to visit China gave a great shock to Japan. To make the matter worse for Satō, China was then engaged in an anti-Japan campaign, clearly targeted at him.

Then another Nixon shock came in August 1971, in the form of a sudden announcement of a new economic policy that included the immediate imposition of a temporary 10-percent surcharge on all imports. This package of measures was an attempt to prop up the U.S. economy, which was suffering from a post–Vietnam War depression, and to improve the U.S. balance of trade, which had become unfavorable for the first time since the end of World War II. With the imposition of the 10-percent surcharge, Nixon aimed to force other developed countries to adjust the exchange rates of their respective currencies to the U.S. dollar. The upshot was the Smithsonian Conference of December 1971, in which the major advanced countries revalued their currencies upward against the dollar. But this proved to be a temporary adjustment. After another adjustment of exchange rates, floating rates were introduced for exchanges between major currencies. These changes in the currency-exchange system did not much affect the competitiveness of Japanese products and the continuing growth of the Japanese economy.

In January 1972, just before Satō's meeting with Nixon in San Clemente, California, Japan and the United States signed a textile trade agreement. The San Clemente summit repaired Japan–U.S. relations, which had been much strained during the previous year. A joint statement issued at that meeting set the date of the Okinawa reversion as May 15 of that year. Soon after the return of Okinawa to Japan, Satō expressed his intention to resign. In July 1972, he was succeeded as prime minister by Kakuei Tanaka.

During Satō's long tenure as prime minister, Japan became a major economic power, surpassing the promise of his predecessor to double the national income. Although Nixon often treated Japan rather harshly, it was because he regarded Japan as a rival as well as an ally. He regarded Japan as one of the five poles in his design of a new world order. He paid his respect to Japan's new status by traveling to Alaska to welcome Emperor Hirohito, who stopped at the Anchorage Airport on his way to Europe. In August 1972, he went to Hawaii—half way to Japan—in order to meet Japan's new prime minister, Kakuei Tanaka. At that meeting, Tanaka promised to let Japanese airlines buy passenger planes from U.S. makers as a means to redress the nations' existing bilateral trade imbalance. Tanaka later involved himself in airplane purchases and illegally took money from the Lockheed Corporation, which sold airplanes to a Japanese airline company.

Zhou Enlai, the prime minister of the People's Republic of China, also recognized Japan's importance, and he decided to hasten the normalization of relations between the two countries. In September 1972, Zhou invited Tanaka to establish diplomatic relations with Japan, which then terminated its official relations with Taiwan. Zhou told Tanaka that China would not object to Japan's security ties with the United States. For many years the People's Republic of China had insisted that Japan–U.S. security relations were incompatible with friendly Japan–China relations. But now it became possible for Japan to develop friendly relations with China while maintaining its security ties with the United States. Thus Nixon's shocking *demarche* turned out to be a great benefit for Japan, because it removed a dilemma from the Japanese diplomatic situation.

When the Fourth Middle Eastern War took place in October 1973, Japan was to experience a great shock of a different kind— a severe shortage of petroleum caused by the oil embargo policy of the Organization of Arab Petroleum Exporting Countries (OAPEC). Panicked by the oil embargo, Japan hurriedly sent its diplomatic missions to OAPEC states to beg them to resume petroleum exports to Japan, revising its position on the Arab–Israel dispute from an even-handed stance to a pro-Arab one. The oil embargo and the hike of crude oil prices strongly impacted the economies of oil-importing countries, putting them into depression.

In 1974, President Nixon tried to prevent the Watergate scandal from engulfing him by endeavoring to convince the American public that he was indispensable as an international statesman for coping with global issues. But in August he was forced to resign in order to avoid an impeachment trial, and Vice-President Gerald Ford succeeded him as president. President Ford came to Japan as a national guest in November 1974. This was the first official visit of a U.S. president to Japan. Emperor Hirohito visited the United States for the first time in 1975. Soon after Ford's visit to Japan, Tanaka resigned as prime minister because of rising public criticism of his alleged involvement in a political scandal (unrelated to the Lockheed scandal). He was succeeded by Takeo Miki, whom the LDP bosses chose as the new leader because of his clean image. It was Miki who decided to indict his predecessor in the Lockheed scandal on the basis of evidence that the U.S. government provided to the Japanese government at his request.

Ford lost to Jimmy Carter in the election of 1976, and Miki resigned after the LDP lost a number of its seats in the lower house election in December of that year. While Carter was in office, Japan had two prime ministers, Takeo Fukuda and Masayoshi Ōhira. Both were former officials of the Ministry of Finance and politicians of considerable wisdom and competence. But they were rivals within the LDP, and the intra-party infighting that resulted because of their rivalry shortened their respective tenures as prime minister.

Fukuda was known for his announcement of that which became known as the Fukuda Doctrine, which pledged Japan's cooperation with the ASEAN countries in various fields and avowed that Japan would never seek to be a military power again. Ōhira was known for his attempt to develop the idea of comprehensive security for Japan, which needed a constant inflow of essential resources from overseas for the welfare of its people.

It is said that Carter failed to get along well with European leaders. However, his relations with Japanese leaders were much better. The Japanese press respected him for his personal integrity and liked his folksy touch. There was some apprehension in Japan regarding his policies on U.S. troops in Korea and on nuclear energy. But these issues were eventually settled in ways that dispelled Japan's apprehension. Also, trade friction over Japanese steel and electric appliances and American oranges and orange juice were kept under control.

In the second half of the 1970s, the economies of both Japan and the United States regained relative prosperity. Japanese companies managed to quickly absorb the great hike in oil prices, and the Japanese economy recovered from depression. The U.S. economy did relatively well until 1979, when the Islamic revolution in Iran resulted in the second petroleum crisis. But because the supply of petroleum from the Middle East did not stop, the Japanese economy managed to absorb the shock of this crisis, which pushed oil prices to their highest level ever.

Toward the end of the 1970s, the world was moving into an era of new international tension, that is, a new phase of the Cold War. In December 1979, the Soviet Union sent armed forces to Afghanistan in order to keep a pro-Soviet government in power there. The U.S.S.R. was trying to retain, as it had done in Hungary and Czechoslovakia, what it regarded as part of the Soviet empire. But the status of Afghanistan in the Cold War had been unclear, and this armed Soviet action alarmed Americans very much, because it seemed to indicate a Soviet ambition to extend its sphere of influence southward toward the Persian Gulf and the Indian Ocean. Indeed, the Soviet Union had been engaged in an expansionist drive in various parts of the Third World during the 1970s, taking advantage of post–Vietnam War American inaction. In

Southeast Asia, the Soviet Union made Vietnam its ally and began making use of naval and air bases in that country, while aiding the latter's military action in Cambodia. To counter the Soviet expansionist drive, in January 1979 the Carter administration formalized the U.S. relationship with the People's Republic of China, relegating its relationship with the Taipei regime to an unofficial one. The next month, China made war against Vietnam for a short while, and in that same year the beginning of the Afghanistan War drove the United States and China closer toward each other.

Japan was a partner of the two countries in their coalition against Soviet expansionism. In August 1978, Japan concluded a treaty of peace and friendship with China, and in October of that year Deng Xiaoping visited Japan and told the Japanese people that it was natural for them to maintain security ties with the United States and to develop Japan's self-defense capability. In December 1979, Japan promised China to expand its economic cooperation with that country through a new program of yen loans. In 1980, Japan began to offer "strategic assistance" to nations such as Thailand, Pakistan, and Turkey, whose respective stability was important to Japan's own national interest. As a gesture of protest against the Soviet invasion of Afghanistan, Japan boycotted the Moscow 1980 Olympic Games.

In the election year of 1980, the Carter administration had to cope with both the Iranian taking of hostages at the U.S. embassy in Teheran and the Soviet invasion of Afghanistan. The Islamic revolution in Iran, which brought anti-American Islamic ayatollahs to power, triggered the second oil crisis and pushed the American economy into depression. In November 1980, when the Carter administration admitted the former-Shah Reza Pahlevi to an American hospital for medical treatment, Iranian radical students occupied the U.S. embassy in Teheran and took a number of American diplomats as hostages. Because the Iranian government did not persuade the students to release the hostages, this hostage affair remained unresolved until the very end of the Carter presidency. Whereas the United States imposed economic sanctions against Iran in retaliation for the taking of hostages, Japan was for a while reluctant to discontinue friendly relations with such a steady supplier of oil to Japan. The Japanese government allowed

Japanese oil companies to continue to import a large quantity of crude oil from Iran. After Washington's strong protest against what it regarded as insensitive Japanese behavior, the Ōhira cabinet quickly brought Japan into line with the United States in regard to economic sanctions against Iran.

In 1980, the American people, much frustrated with the U.S. economic downturn, the prolonged Teheran hostage affair, and Soviet expansionist drives in the Third World, were craving for a turn of the tide and therefore a new leader. The Republican candidate Ronald Reagan, who had been a critic of détente with the Soviet Union, in his election campaign pledged to voters to restore America to its former position of might, and he defeated the incumbent president in the election, held in November.

In June 1980, Prime Minister Ōhira died of a heart attack while campaigning in a general election that he had been forced to call when a no-confidence resolution was passed in the lower house because of the absence of the Fukuda faction. His sudden death resulted in Zenkō Suzuki becoming the prime minister. Because Suzuki belonged to the same political faction as Ōhira, he was expected to carry on his predecessor's policies. But he lacked capabilities comparable to those of Ōhira. When Suzuki visited Washington in May 1981 to meet Reagan, the two leaders declared in a joint statement that "the alliance between the United States and Japan is built upon their shared values of democracy and liberty . . . ." This was the first time that the term *alliance* was used in a joint statement of the top leaders of Japan and America. Suzuki also announced in a speech in Washington that Japan would extend its capability to defend sea lanes. However, when Japanese reporters asked him about the significance of using the term *alliance* in the joint declaration, the prime minister stated that the Japan–U.S. alliance did not have any military connotation. He even complained that bureaucrats had not adequately consulted with him in drafting the joint declaration. That statement caused Foreign Minister Masayoshi Itō to resign.

This episode revealed Suzuki's incompetence. But it also reflected the fact that for many years the Japanese government had tended both to deemphasize the aspect of bilateral military cooperation in its presentation of Japan–U.S. security relations to the public and to limit Japan's military role to the minimum. While Suzuki damaged his credibility by statements unbecoming a prime minister, his new Foreign Minister Sunao Sonoda did not get along well with American officials. The Suzuki cabinet shortened its life by its mishandling of Japan–U.S. relations. Suzuki decided to resign as prime minister without seeking reelection when his term as LDP president came to end. In November 1982, he was succeeded by a more-colorful, more-self-assertive leader, Yasuhiro Nakasone.

Nakasone had been known as a nationalist when in his 30s and 40s. He was still a nationalist, but he identified Japan as a member of the Western alliance in general and as America's ally in particular. He believed that Japan, as one of the advanced Western-alliance countries, should play an international role commensurate with its economic power. He did not hesitate to discuss military matters with Western leaders. While in Washington, he reportedly used the military metaphor "unsinkable aircraft carrier" to describe Japan's military role in the northwestern Pacific. During his tenure, Nakasone dealt with a number of problems in Japan–U.S. relations, such as the development of Japan's sea-lane defense capability, the transfer of Japanese militarily applicable technologies to the United States, and the cooperation of Japanese firms in SDI-related projects. Reagan welcomed Nakasone's advent to Japan's leadership and developed a personal friendship with him, which in Japanese journalism was referred to as "the Ron–Yasu relationship."

Nakasone also tried hard to reduce Japan's trade imbalance with the United States. After Japanese car makers began to voluntarily restrict their exports of automobile to the United States in 1981, Japan–U.S. trade friction shifted from the issue of such voluntary restrictions to the issue of removing invisible barriers to the Japanese domestic market so as to make it more accessible to American goods and services. Under Nakasone's leadership, in July 1985 the Japanese government adopted an action program for increasing foreign access to Japan's markets. In the next year, a group commissioned by Nakasone submitted a paper known as the Maekawa Report, which stressed the need to improve the openness of Japan's domestic markets. But Japan was slow to remove invisible barriers, because they were intertwined with the vested interests of bureaucracies, industries, and politicians. In September 1985, Japan joined the G-5 agreement to lower the exchange rate of the U.S. dollar vis-à-vis other major currencies. This measure helped to restrain the growth of the U.S.–Japan trade imbalance. But it stimulated what seemed to Americans to be another kind of Japanese economic invasion. As the value of yen went up greatly, Japanese makers were encouraged to build factories or to buy American companies so that Japanese products for the American market would be produced within the United States itself. Japanese investors also began to invest in real estate, including some well-known pieces of real estate like the Rockefeller Plaza in New York.

Although the leaders of the two countries were on friendly terms, U.S. public resentment was mounting against Japan, which seemed to guard its home market while liberally invading other countries' markets. This resentment exploded in April 1987, when it became known that the Toshiba Machine Company, a subsidiary of the Toshiba Corporation, had illegally exported submarine screws to the Soviet Union, violating the CoCom regulations. Many Americans alleged that this export had helped the Soviet navy make its submarines more difficult to detect and caused great damage to the national security of the United States. In an anti-Japanese gesture, several congressmen used sledge hammers to destroy Toshiba products. The next year, the U.S. Congress enacted a new trade act, the Comprehensive Trade Act of 1988. This act strengthened America's power to retaliate against unfair trade practices. It also included provisions for punishing the Toshiba Machine Co. and the Toshiba Corporation for the former's illegal export of submarine screws. The phenomenon called "Japan bashing" began to thrive in the United States. A number of American authors described Japan as an economic juggernaut that was undermining the economic power of the United States. They regarded Japan as a new menace that was more formidable than the Soviet Union, whose challenge seemed to be winding down. They described Japanese economic expansion in such terms as *invasion, conquest, occupation*, and the like.

Meanwhile, many Japanese became arrogant in their attitude towards the United States, which they regarded as a declining giant or a country suffering from serious internal troubles. Many

Japanese felt that they no longer had anything to learn from America. Even Prime Minister Nakasone, who took pride in his reputation as an international statesman, caused a storm of protest in the United States by his remark that mono-ethnic Japan was a more intelligent society than was multiethnic America. Of course he hurried to control the damage from that remark by expressing his apology and by reiterating his respect for the United States. But his remark revealed that he was lacking in his understanding of the new multiethnic America.

Nakasone retired from office after five years as prime minister, in November 1987. He nominated Noboru Takeshita as his successor to the LDP presidency, resulting in Takeshita becoming prime minister. Takeshita, a master of interest-group politics, was able to stay in power for only one and one-half years because of his involvement in a scandal. After Nakasone, only one Japanese prime minister has remained in office for as long as two and one-half years; all of the others held the position for less than two years. As weak cabinets, LDP-centered or otherwise, took turns leading Japan, the country began to sink into a long period of economic stagnation.

5. JAPAN–U.S. RELATIONS AFTER THE COLD WAR

When revisionist views of Japan became popular in the United States, the Cold War was ending. Mikhail Gorbachev, who became the leader of the Soviet Union in March 1985, surprised the world by introducing "new thinking" into its diplomacy and "*perestroica*" and "*glasnost*" into its domestic policy. President Reagan, who had criticized the Soviet Union as an evil empire a few years before, welcomed Gorbachev's brave attempts at change. In December 1987, the two leaders signed the Intermediate-Range Nuclear Forces (INF) Treaty, which required the destruction of all intermediate-range missiles possessed by the two countries.

But the momentum for change did not stop at a partial restructuring of the Soviet political economy and a reorientation of Soviet diplomacy toward international accommodation. In 1989, the Communist system collapsed under overwhelming popular demand for democracy in Soviet-bloc countries one after another. In Germany, the Berlin Wall, the symbol of the Cold War divide, was destroyed. Gorbachev stoically accepted this series of great changes in Central and Eastern Europe. In December 1989, Gorbachev and George Bush, Reagan's successor, met in Malta and declared the end of the Cold War. The Western world was thrilled with this great change in the Soviet Union and its satellite nations. However, although the West praised Gorbachev's leadership in bringing about this great change, he was losing popular support at home because of economic disruptions and separatist movements. He would eventually fail to ride out the difficult situation, and on December 25, 1991, he resigned as president of the Soviet Union, which on that same day ceased to exist.

During the spring of the eventful year 1989, the wind for democratic change seemed to be blowing also in the People's Republic of China. Students occupied Tiananmen Square in Beijing, demanding the government to institute democratic reforms. Zhao Ziyang, the number-two leader of the Communist Party, had a conciliatory dialogue with student activists. But early in June, Deng Xiaoping, a firm believer in reform from above, but not from below, who in 1987 had removed Hu Yaoban, his former right-hand man, from the number-two post because of pro-democratic deviation, decided to crush the democratic movement with armed forces and to oust the weak-minded Zhao from the number-two post. Western countries condemned the Chinese leadership for the resulting Tiananmen massacre and in protest downgraded their relations with China. The United States and Japan, two major countries with close relations with China, distanced themselves from that country, curtailing their respective cooperative relations. But Japan took care to retain its position as the G-7 country most friendly or least unfriendly toward China. In summit meetings of the G-7 countries, Japan defended its posture towards China, emphasizing the long-term need to keep China within the international community. The U.S. government, too, was very much aware of the necessity of engaging China. As Secretary of State James Baker later wrote in his memoir, "Overriding strategic interests of the United States require engagement, not isolation." The U.S. government's reaction was milder than that of the U.S. public. It renewed China's most-favored-nation status in spite of considerable opposition in Congress. It sent two high-ranking officials on a secret mission to Beijing in December 1989 to convey its interest in a constructive relationship with China. When their mission became known to the public, it was criticized in Congress as kow-tow diplomacy. Japan, as the country most friendly toward China at that time, had special value for China. A move by Japan toward normal relations with China would certainly have a positive influence on the attitude of Western countries toward China. Therefore, the Chinese government was interested in inviting the Japanese emperor and his wife to China. From the viewpoint of the Japanese government, too, it was good timing for the royal couple to visit China when the Chinese government most eagerly wanted their visit. Thus, Emperor Akihito and Empress Michiko visited China in October 1992, symbolizing normalization of the relations of the two countries.

For several years after the Tiananmen incident, China kept a low profile in international affairs, waiting for relations with Western countries to normalize, while pursing a policy of economic growth and keeping its door open to foreign capital. During the Gulf crisis of 1990–91, China went along with a U.N. Security Council consensus that had been forged under U.S. leadership. But it was that Middle Eastern crisis that broadened the psychological gap between Japanese and Americans.

When in early August 1990, Iraq, under Saddam Hussein's rule, invaded Kuwait and announced the annexation of that country, the U.N. Security Council condemned this aggression and demanded Iraq to restore the previous status quo. The Bush administration responded forcefully to the Iraqi invasion, regarding it as an open challenge to the "new world order" and as a bold leap in Iraq's quest for regional hegemony. The United States, together with a number of nations acting pursuant to a resolution of the U.N. Security Council, sent armed forces to Saudi Arabia and the Persian Gulf so as to insure Saudi Arabia's security and to pressure Hussein to accept the Security Council's resolutions. Because Hussein refused to accede, in November 1990 the United States greatly increased its forces in the Gulf region.

At the beginning of the Gulf crisis, Japan's diplomatic response was slow and characterized by inaction—strange as that was for a nation that depended on the Gulf region for most of its supply of crude oil, which was vital to the nation. But Japan's passivity reflected a continuation of what had been the nation's usual stance in the past. Japan had been indifferent to international crises in the Middle East. Because Japan's interest in that region had been based on keeping a steady inflow of crude oil, Japan had not much bothered itself about wars in the Middle East as long as they did not disturb the oil supply to Japan. Because Japan had enjoyed an abundant supply of crude oil during the decade-long Iran–Iraqi War, the new crisis did not alarm the Japanese. As a peace-minded nation, Japan should have seriously considered the implications that the Iraqi aggression had for world peace. But this peace-minded nation had been very inward-looking, interested primarily in avoiding involvement in foreign wars during the several decades since the end of World War II. Thus unaccustomed to playing an active role in meeting threats to international peace and security, Japan—though having the world's second-largest economy and being an affluent partner of the United States—was very slow to decide what it could and should do in response to this post–Cold War crisis.

The Japanese government headed by Prime Minister Toshiki Kaifu was of course willing for Japan to participate in U.N.-sponsored economic sanctions against Iraq. But it took four weeks for Japan to announce what else Japan would do in support of the international action to enforce the U.N. resolutions. Toward the end of August 1991, the Japanese government announced its plan to cooperate with the international activities in the Gulf region through nonmilitary means. The plan included a contribution of $1 billion to support the international police action there.

The announcement of the Japanese plan disappointed Americans and was criticized by them as too meager. Surprised by the American criticism, the Japanese government announced in mid-September that Japan would contribute $2 billion to help the Gulf states and would add $1 billion to its support of the international police action. But that did little to change the American impression that in an international crisis Japan was an unworthy ally.

In this situation, the Kaifu cabinet and LDP Diet members regret-
ted that Japan was not able under its existing law to send its
Self-Defense Forces overseas to participate in an international
police action to enforce U.N. Security Council resolutions. In
October 1990, the government submitted to the Diet a bill to allow
Japanese personnel to be sent overseas for noncombat activities in
support of international peacekeeping operations based on U.N.
resolutions. But the government gave up the bill because of a lack
of support among the opposition parties (the LDP lacked a majority in the upper house).

Because it was impossible for the United States to keep a formidable military force in the Gulf region indefinitely, in January 1991
the Bush administration obtained from the U.N. Security Council
a resolution authorizing member states to use force against Iraq to
liberate Kuwait. The Gulf crisis developed into war that same
month, when coalition forces attacked Iraqi forces. The war ended
four weeks later, when Iraq accepted all of the Security Council's
conditions for an armistice. After the beginning of the Gulf War,
the Japanese government declared that Japan would contribute an
additional $9 billion dollars in support of the multinational forces
in the Gulf region, and it obtained the approval of the Diet to do
so. That brought the total of Japan's Gulf-related financial contributions to $13 billion, including $2 billion in economic assistance.
Inasmuch as the total cost of the war was $71 billion, of which the
United States contributed $7.4 billion, the Japanese financial con-
tribution was very substantial. In the fury of war, the international
community did not much recognize the financial contributions of
Japan, whose forces did not participate in the multinational coalition. To compensate for the absence of Japanese in the coalition
forces, Japan sent several mine-sweepers to the Persian Gulf after
the war was over.

The Gulf War—the first regional war of the post–Cold War
era—revealed psychological gaps between the United States and
Japan. The Japanese people felt frustrated, believing that Japan
had been asked to underwrite a military operation regarding
which it had not been consulted. They also felt that their financial
contributions were not adequately appreciated by Americans.
Because of their peace culture, Japanese were unable to share the

American enthusiasm over the military victory. On the other side, Americans felt let down by Tokyo's slow response and the seeming indifference of the Japanese public to the crisis. Americans did not appreciate Japan's slow and piecemeal announcements of financial contributions, and they felt that Japan did not do enough, not sending even noncombat forces to the Gulf region. To Americans, Japan seemed to be a mere money machine that needed to be kicked hard before even starting to contribute money.

All in all, Tokyo contributed to the cause of the international community on a scale appropriate to a major economic power in the category in which it was strong, while Washington provided the international community with diplomatic leadership and military power. Although the Gulf crisis revealed gaps in the psychologies of the two nations, it can be said that they both contributed—each in the fields in which it was able to mobilize its respective resources most effectively—to achieving a common goal.

The experience of the Gulf crisis taught the Japanese a lesson: A peace-oriented civilian power should not merely avoid international conflicts, but should do something to contribute to the cause of international peace and order. After the war, because two opposition parties, the Kōmei Party and the Democratic Socialist Party, seemed to favor sending Self-Defense Forces to U.N.-sponsored peacekeeping operations under strict conditions, in September 1991 the government introduced a bill to permit that. But the bill did not go through the Diet quickly. After Kiichi Miyazawa became prime minister, replacing Kaifu, who had been criticized for his weak leadership, the bill was finally enacted in June 1992 as the International Peace Cooperation Act. In order to obtain the consent of the Kōmei Party, it was agreed that, for the time being, any Self-Defense Forces that were dispatched would be limited to support activities. This law immediately opened the way for Japan's participation in peacekeeping operations in Cambodia. Because Japan had played an active diplomatic role in bringing a peace settlement to that country, the Japanese government particularly wanted a visible participation in peacekeeping in Cambodia (Japan sent 600 Self-Defense Forces personnel, plus civilian policemen and private volunteers). Later, much smaller units of Self-Defense Forces personnel were dispatched to several other places, such as Mozambique and the Golan Heights.

In spite of the psychological gap between Tokyo and Washington during the Gulf affair, in the end the United States certainly was satisfied with Japan's total financial contributions, and Japan certainly appreciated what the diplomatic and military leadership of the United States had accomplished for the international community and oil-importing countries. Thus, both governments emphasized the importance of Japan–U.S. cooperation in the post–Cold War era. The year of the 50th anniversary of Japan's attack on Pearl Harbor passed without any flare-up of anti-Japanese feelings in the United States. In a November 1991 speech in New York, President Bush noted that Japan was supporting U.S. military forces in Japan with $3 billion in annual host-nation contributions. He also praised Japan for its contribution of $13 billion to the multinational forces during the Gulf War, specifically mentioning that $10 billion of that money went to the United States. When Bush made speeches at Pearl Harbor and in Honolulu on December 7, he stated that former-enemy countries now stood with the United States for democracy and called upon Japan to join the United States "in a future energized by free markets and free peoples." As this last remark suggested, Bush was trying to open Asian markets, particularly the Japanese market, more widely for American products and services. Before his departure for an Asia-Pacific tour towards the end of 1991, the president explained that the primary purpose of his tour was to create jobs for Americans. Because the American economy was in a slump, Bush emphasized the aim of creating employment for Americans at home by increasing U.S. exports to Asian markets. When as part of the tour he visited Japan early in January 1992, he was accompanied by executives of America's "Big Three" auto makers. Bush was particularly interested in facilitating sales of American cars and auto parts in Japan. Negotiations in Tokyo produced a document called "A Joint-Action Program for a Japan–U.S. Global Partnership," pursuant to which Japan agreed to take a variety of measures to improve access to the Japanese market for American products and services. The document listed a number of measures to be taken by the Japanese government and the Japanese automobile industry with regard to automobiles and auto parts. But these measures were not effective enough to satisfy the American side, and friction over automobile and auto parts trade did not cease, reaching a climax in June 1995.

Because the American economy did not improve in 1992, President Bush was defeated by the Democratic candidate Bill Clinton in the presidential election of that year. The Democrats thus captured the White House for the first time since 1980. President Clinton took the view that economic issues had become increasingly important in post–Cold War international relations, and he therefore decided to take a tougher stance than his predecessors toward Japan on trade issues. When Prime Minister Miyazawa visited Washington in April 1993, the new president told him that because the Cold War partnership was outmoded it was necessary to change U.S.–Japan relations. The Clinton administration wanted the Japanese government to agree on numerical targets for increasing the sale in Japan of certain American products, particularly auto parts. Although the Japanese government did not accept the idea of numerical targets, Prime Minister Miyazawa wished to reach some agreement on trade issues during the Tokyo G-7 summit meeting in July 1993. After much discussion, the two leaders agreed on a framework for a new economic partnership. In their joint declaration, they announced that a set of "objective criteria" would be established to assess progress in each sectoral and structural area.

When Miyazawa made this agreement with Clinton, the life of his cabinet was in imminent danger because of the defection of the Ozawa–Hata faction from the LDP. In the general election held one week later, the LDP lost its majority in the lower house and its position as the ruling party for the first time since 1955. But also remarkable was that the Social Democrats (formerly the Socialist Party) were much weakened as a result of the election. A coalition government headed by Morihiro Hosokawa, a former governor of Kumamoto Prefecture who had organized a new party called the New Japan Party, came into power. Clinton welcomed this change and expected the new prime minister to break the power of Japan's stonewalling bureaucracy and to liberalize the country's political economy. But the two governments became deadlocked on the issue of establishing numerical targets. While the American side interpreted the Miyazawa–Clinton agreement on objective criteria as agreement on numerical targets, the Japanese side resisted the idea of such targets. Tokyo feared that Washington would regard numerical targets as Japanese commitments and might retaliate if the targets were not attained, as it had done in the case of an earlier agreement regarding semiconductors. In a meeting held in Washington in February 1994, Clinton and Hosokawa failed to break the deadlock.

*　　*　　*

Two months later, Hosokawa suddenly resigned as prime minister when he was criticized by the LDP for a minor political scandal. Tsutomu Hata of the New Life Party inherited the position of leader of the coalition government, but soon the coalition collapsed because the Social Democrats opposed the attempt of other coalition groups to merge into a single party called the New Frontier Party. This gave the LDP a chance to return to power. The LDP formed a coalition with the Social Democratic Party and the Harbinger Party, and gave the post of the prime minister to the Social Democratic leader Tomiichi Murayama, although a majority of the cabinet posts went to LDP members. It was quite ironic that a Social Democrat became Japan's prime minister when the strength of the Social Democratic Party itself was declining steeply. When the Social Democrats had joined in a coalition government headed by Prime Minister Hosokawa, they had temporarily suspended their traditional opposition to the Self-Defense Forces and to the Japan–U.S. Security Treaty. But Prime Minister Murayama now declared that the Self-Defense Forces were constitutional and that Japan should maintain its security relations with the United States. The Social Democrats adopted Murayama's position on these issues as their own.

The Murayama cabinet had to cope with the unresolved trade dispute with the Clinton administration. In May 1995, U.S. Trade Representative (USTR) Michael Kantor announced that the U.S. government would impose 100-percent duties on imports of Japanese luxury cars if Japan did not agree to take appropriate measures to remove impediments to the sale of American auto parts and automotive accessories in Japan before the deadline of June 28. The Japanese government appealed the case to the World Trade Organization and declared that Japan would retaliate if the United States were to impose sanctions. Meanwhile, Kantor and Ryūtarō Hashimoto, Japan's minister of international trade and industry, engaged in tough negotiations in Geneva to attempt to settle the dispute so as to avoid a trade war between the two nations. Although Hashimoto proposed a number of measures to stimulate sales of American automobiles and auto parts in Japan, he refused to commit the Japanese government to numerical targets. Because a trade war was no more desired by the United States than by Japan, and because a WTO decision might not favor the United States, Kantor finally decided to accept a compromise resolution that did not include numerical targets. Although in the two leaders' joint statements Kantor estimated how much the sale of automobiles and auto parts would increase due to specific measures, Hashimoto made it clear in the same documents that the Japanese government was not involved in the USTR's estimates. With this agreement, the most serious Japan–U.S. trade dispute of the Clinton era was settled.

In the second half of the 1990s, the United States continued to complain about the Japanese economy. But the tone and nature of the complaint changed greatly. While the American economy was enjoying a great boom in the era of global capitalism, the Japanese economy, which had declined in 1992, remained stagnant throughout the 1990s. In the second half of that decade, Americans no longer spoke of Japan's economic power as a threat. The Japanese economy seemed to be a problem, not a threat. The United States began to exhort Japan to resume its economic growth so that its home market could absorb more American products.

Prime Minister Murayama left his mark in a historic document, his statement as Japan's prime minister on the 50th anniversary of the end of World War II. In that statement Murayama stressed that "we must look to the past to learn from the lessons of history and to ensure that we do not stray from the path of peace and prosperity in the future." He noted that "Japan, following a mistaken national policy, advanced along the road to war, only to ensnare the Japanese people in a fateful crisis, and through its colonial rule and aggression, caused tremendous damage and suffering to the peoples of many countries, particularly to those of Asian nations." He then expressed "my feelings of deep remorse" and "my heartfelt apology" for "these irrefutable facts of history." He also expressed his gratitude to the countries of the world, especially to the United States, which had helped the Japanese to rebuild their nation after the war. Any prime minister would have made a similar statement in that occasion. But a Liberal Democratic prime minister might have watered down a number of phrases under pressure from those who argued that Japan had not been a particularly bad villain in World War II.

In the middle of the 1990s, a controversy developed in Japan over a historical exhibit planned for inclusion among the permanent exhibits of the Peace Prayer Hall to be built by government funding. Although the prayer hall was a project of the Ministry of Welfare, the project's real sponsor was the Japan War-Bereaved Families Association. When the content of the planned exhibit became known, many historians criticized it because it seemed to justify Japan's road to World War II, and the Ministry of Welfare eventually eliminated the controversial historical exhibit from the project. Meanwhile, Murayama visited Southeast Asian countries in August 1994, and realized how important it was for Japan to study its modern history in an international context. Thus, he launched the Peace, Friendship and Exchange Initiative. As referred to in Murayama's 50th anniversary statement, mentioned above, the initiative consisted of two parts: support for historical research regarding relations between modern Japan and countries in Asia and elsewhere, and rapid expansion of exchange programs with those countries. Although funding for this initiative has been modest, it remains as a valuable legacy of Murayama's premiership.

In the United States, too, war history became a political issue—over an *Enola Gay* exhibit planned by the National Air and Space Museum, one of the museums of the Smithsonian Institution. Because 1995 was the 50th anniversary of the atomic bombing of Hiroshima, the museum planned to display the *Enola Gay*. But along with that airplane was to be a historical exhibit that would include pictures of the devastated city and suffering people. The exhibit was intended to motivate viewers to think about the meaning of the atomic bombing of Hiroshima. But because U.S. veterans' organizations criticized the planned exhibit for throwing doubt on the justice of the patriotic mission of the *Enola Gay*, the plan for the exhibit became a matter of public controversy. Public opinion was mainly critical of the museum, maintaining that an exhibit in a publicly funded museum should not reflect the private views of its curator. In September 1994, the U.S. Senate adopted an resolution that the *Enola Gay* exhibit "should reflect appropriate sensitivity toward the men and women who faithfully and selflessly served the United States during World War II and should avoid impugning the memory of those who gave their lives for freedom." As a result of such public pressure, the National Air and Space Museum discarded its plan for the historical exhibit.

This result was disappointing to the Japanese. The Japanese tended to view the atomic bombings of Hiroshima and Nagasaki as acts in and of themselves, separating them from the general context of World War II. They tended to regard those events only with the mentality of a victim. In contrast, Americans tended to view the bombings in the general context of the war, and with the mentality of a victor. For them, those bombings were part of a glorious victory in an honorable war. The U.S. Postal Service revealed this victor mentality when, to commemorate the end of World War II, it planned to print postal stamps depicting an atomic-explosion's mushroom cloud. But because Japan complained about the planned stamp, the White House put pressure on the Postal Service, inducing the latter to drop the plan.

It is desirable for the two nations to narrow the gap in their perception of the atomic bombings by respectively developing more-encompassing views regarding those events. The Japanese should view the atomic bombings in the context of World War II as a whole, which included Japan's aggression in China, the Tripartite Pact, and the attack on Pearl Harbor. They could then ask Americans to view the atomic bombings themselves as tragic, inhumane acts.

✳   ✳   ✳

Within the Clinton administration, there were people, like
Assistant Secretary of Defense Joseph Nye, who feared that U.S.
confrontationist tactics in trade friction with Japan were undermining the strength of the security ties between the two countries.
Nye was the chief author of a report, published in February
1995, concerning the Clinton administration's security strategy
for the Asia-Pacific region. This report not only announced the
administration's policy of continuing the forward deployment of
U.S. troops to preserve international peace and security in the
region, but also declared its commitment to maintaining the
existing level of 100,000 troops in that area. Given this strategic
posture of the United States, America's security alliance with
Japan was "the linchpin of U.S. security policy in Asia." The
United States therefore had "no more important bilateral relationship" than the one it had with Japan. When Nye had visited
Japan in the previous year, he sensed that the Japanese, disen-
chanted with the United States due to Clinton's unidimensional
emphasis on trade issues, were groping for a multilateral framework for Japan's future security. The report of Japan's Advisory
Group on Defense Issues, "The Modality of the Security and
Defense Capability of Japan," which was submitted to Prime
Minister Murayama in August 1994, seemed to Nye to reveal
such a trend. Feeling the need to revitalize bilateral security ties
between the two nations, Nye initiated a series of intergovernmental dialogues for that purpose.

No matter what interest Japan had in developing a multilateral
security framework, there was wider support among the Japanese
people for the Japan–U.S. Security Treaty than before. Among the
political parties with considerable strength, only the Communist
Party was opposed to the treaty. International tensions had not disappeared in East Asia with the end of the Cold War, and there were
uncertainties in Japan's international environment. North Korea
seemed to pose for Japan an increasingly serious security problem,
because it was developing missiles and was suspected of making
nuclear weapons. Japan did not possess military means to counter
such developments nor diplomatic resources to induce that
unfriendly neighbor to restrain its military programs. Japan had to
depend upon the strength of the United States to meet this kind of

potential threat. Most Japanese therefore felt that Japan should maintain its security ties with the United States for the foreseeable future.

When the Kantor–Hashimoto agreement reduced the conflict over trade issues, the Japanese government desired to reestablish U.S.–Japan relations on the basis of firm bilateral security ties. Because President Clinton was expected to participate in the APEC Conference in Osaka in November 1995, that seemed likely to be a good occasion for the U.S. president and Japan's prime minister to issue a joint declaration reaffirming cooperative relations between the two countries. But this plan did not materialize, because President Clinton was compelled to stay in Washington for domestic reasons. The presidential visit was postponed to April 1996. In January 1996, Prime Minister Murayama resigned as prime minister to give the leadership of a coalition government to Ryūtarō Hashimoto, the president of the largest party in the coalition.

✳   ✳   ✳

There was one problem to which both the Japanese and the U.S. governments had to pay special attention in their discussion of security cooperation. That concerned the desire of the Okinawan people for the U.S. military presence in Okinawa to be reduced. In September 1995, an elementary school girl was raped by three U.S. Marines. This incident enraged the Okinawans, who had endured offenses of this kind for many years, and it rekindled their anti-military-base feelings. Nearly 75 percent of the U.S. military facilities in Japan were located in Okinawa, occupying much of the land on that prefecture's main island. The scale of the U.S. military presence in Okinawa had remained basically the same since the reversion of Okinawa in 1972. The Okinawans felt that while the Japanese people on the nation's main islands had enjoyed mostly the benefits of the security treaty, the Okinawans had been almost alone in suffering from the disadvantages of that treaty. Although it can be argued that the Okinawans, too, benefited from the existence of U.S. military bases, because the bases created many jobs for Okinawans, they were tired of living with the U.S. military presence.

The Legislative Assembly of Okinawa Prefecture adopted a resolution that demanded the U.S. military to tighten the discipline of
its personnel and to prevent the recurrence of offenses against
Okinawans, and it called on the two governments to scale down
the U.S. military presence in Okinawa. Masahide Ōta, the governor
of Okinawa, declared that he would not sign lease-renewal contracts on behalf of landowners who refused to sign contracts to
continue the use of their properties for U.S. military facilities.
Because there had been a group of anti-base landowners who
refused to renew their contracts, the Japanese national government
had adopted a policy of requesting the governor of Okinawa to
sign renewal contracts on their behalf in such cases. Before Ōta was
elected governor, he had been known as a university professor
opposed to the presence of U.S. military bases in Okinawa. He had
hoped that the number of U.S. military bases would be reduced as
a result of the end of the Cold War, but he was disappointed by
Washington's decision to maintain the forward deployment of
100,000 U.S. troops in the East-Asia/Western Pacific region. In view
of the recent unfortunate incident and the subsequent rise of an
anti-U.S.-base movement, the governor decided on this tactic of
contract-renewal refusal as a means of putting strong pressure on
the national government to reduce the scale of the U.S. military
presence in Okinawa. Later the national government prevented the
expiration of the lease contracts by enacting a new law that allowed
the prime minister to sign a lease-renewal contract if the governor's
signature could not be obtained.

Both Murayama and Hashimoto were sympathetic to the desire
of the Okinawans and wanted to do whatever they could do for
them. Several minor steps were soon taken to transfer some U.S.
military facilities and activities from Okinawa to other parts of
Japan. When Hashimoto took over as prime minister after
Murayama, he began to search for more dramatic ways to reduce
the Okinawans' feelings of irritation and frustration. He was eager
to redefine Japan's alliance with the United States. He also wanted
to do something dramatic to please the Okinawan people. Through
his conversations with Ōta, Hashimoto understood that removal
of the U.S. Marines helicopter base at Futenma was what the governor wanted most. Hashimoto cautiously tried to find out if it was

possible to remove the Futenma base, which was located in a dense-ly populated area of the main Okinawan island. He thought that if the base could be moved to a more-peripheral, less-populated place in Okinawa, the Okinawans would be very pleased and would be more supportive of the U.S. military presence. Ambassador Walter F. Mondale supported Hashimoto's effort. In Washington, Secretary of Defense William J. Perry and other Defense Department officials concerned with redefining Japan–U.S. security relations were also pondering the feasibility of moving the Futenma base. President Clinton and Defense Department officials were pleased with the appearance of the new prime minister who, though a tough nego-tiator in trade disputes, was known as a reliable friend in security affairs. Because of Washington's cooperative attitude toward Hashimoto, the two governments were able to agree before Clinton's visit on the removal of the helicopter base from Futenma.

In the early months of 1996, serious tension developed in the Taiwan Straits when the People's Republic of China staged a mili-tary maneuver of considerable scale in the straits in an attempt to intimidate the Taiwanese people, who were going to hold their first democratic presidential election in March. The United States sent two aircraft carriers near Taiwan to convey to Beijing America's strong disapproval of the use of force against Taiwan. It was like-ly that China's threatening tactics in this crisis strengthened the Japanese people's support of their security alliance with the United States.

In the middle of April 1996, President Clinton made a state visit to Japan. After his talks with Prime Minister Hashimoto, the two leaders issued "A Joint Declaration on Security" on April 17. It was a formal declaration that confirmed the determination of the two governments to maintain the bilateral security alliance in the post–Cold War era. Prime Minister Hashimoto and President Clinton reaffirmed that the "Japan–U.S. security relationship remains the cornerstone for achieving common security objectives, and for maintaining a stable and prosperous environment for the Asia-Pacific region as we enter the twenty-first century." They agreed that "the most effective framework for the defense of Japan is close defense cooperation between the two countries" and also that the bilateral security relationship "forms an essential pillar which supports the positive regional engagement of the United States."

While the president reaffirmed the policy of maintaining about 100,000 forward-deployed military personnel in the region, including the current troop level in Japan, the prime minister reconfirmed that Japan would continue appropriate contributions for maintaining U.S. troops in Japan. They agreed to make efforts for enhancing "the credibility of this vital security relationship," and agreed specifically to initiate a review of the 1978 Guidelines for Japan–U.S. Defense Cooperation, to update it. They also defined regional and global cooperation between the two countries on the basis of the Japan–U.S. alliance. Thus, this declaration outlined the relationship of the two countries as that of allies closely cooperating to achieve common purposes.

The joint Hashimoto–Clinton declaration reflected their shared sensitivity and concern regarding local problems in Okinawa. It stated "they agreed that both governments will make every effort to deal with various issues related to the presence and status of U.S. forces." The two leaders "reconfirmed their determination to carry out steps to consolidate, realign, and lessen U.S. facilities and areas consistent with the objectives" of the security treaty. It is also noteworthy that the joint declaration stated more emphatically than previous ones "the profound common values" that guided the respective policies of the two nations: "the maintenance of freedom, the pursuit of democracy, and respect for human rights."

In the spring of 1996, Hashimoto was in an upbeat mood. In retrospect, it was his finest hour. He had reestablished the Japan–U.S. alliance, which had been disrupted by trade disputes. He had secured U.S. consent to remove the helicopter base from Futenma, which he hoped would lessen the resentment of Okinawans toward the excessive concentration of U.S. bases in their prefecture (Later, in December 1996, the two governments agreed to reduce the land allocated for U.S. military facilities in Okinawa by 20 percent. But their agreement that the Futenma base was to be replaced by a new base to be constructed offshore of Nago City did not please the Okinawans. The replacement project has been suspended because Okinawa Prefecture insists that use of the new military base should be limited to 15 years.) . Also, he was not very worried about the Japanese economy, which had been in post-bubble stagnation, because he thought that it was on the road to recovery. He enjoyed ample public approval ratings because of his leadership.

By 1998, however, Hashimoto's popularity plummeted steeply because of the economic recession that started in 1997, and he was forced to resign as prime minister after the LDP's poor performance in the upper house election in 1998. The Clinton administration began to criticize the economic policies of the Japanese government when the Japanese economy went into recession after the consumption tax was raised from three percent to five percent in May 1997. Then, in the autumn of 1997, Yamaichi Securities, one of Japan's "Big Four" securities companies, and the Hokkaido Takushoku Bank, one of the nation's major banks, successively went bankrupt. These incidents were shocking not only to the Japanese people but to the international community in general. American economists and politicians feared for a while that a serious depression might spread from Japan to other parts of the world, putting the entire world into turmoil. Although the Hashimoto cabinet took several measures to save other banks and to put Japan's banking system in order, those actions were not enough to restore the soundness of the Japanese economy and to put it on the path to recovery. Accordingly, Clinton administration officials continued to criticize the economic policies of the Hashimoto cabinet. Although in September 1997 Japan and the United States agreed on new guidelines for bilateral defense cooperation, which, significantly, included cooperation to meet emergency situations in areas surrounding Japan, security cooperation with Japan was not an important concern for the Clinton administration in his second term. Secretary Perry and other Defense Department officials who had worked to redefine the U.S.–Japanese alliance did not remain in the Clinton administration during his second term. Regarding the Asia-Pacific region, Washington focused its attention on two problems: U.S.–Chinese rapprochement and the financial crises in Asian countries. Because of these financial crises, Treasury Department officials, such as Secretary Robert Rubin and Deputy-Secretary Lawrence Summers, played prominent roles in Japan–U.S. relations.

*   *   *

One of Clinton's top diplomatic agenda items for his second term was to repair U.S.–Chinese relations, which had cooled since the Tienanmen incident. During his election campaign in 1992, Clinton had criticized the Bush administration's China policy and had advocated putting greater pressure on Beijing regarding human-rights issues. His attempt to link human rights issues with most-favored-nation trade status for China failed when Beijing refused to improve human-rights conditions in response to Washington's threat of economic sanctions. Because American businesses were keen to enter the expanding Chinese market, the United States government did not have sufficient bargaining power for such a policy to succeed. In 1994, Clinton ceased coupling those two issues, stating that he would try to improve human-rights conditions in China through a policy of engagement. When China began military maneuvers in the Taiwan Straits in January 1996, Clinton dispatched two aircraft carriers to the sea near Taiwan as a warning. It was desirable for him to explain U.S. policy regarding Taiwan to China's leader directly. Because in the 1990s China was achieving impressive economic growth, it was all the more important for the United States to develop a constructive relationship with that nation, a country with superpower potential. Clinton planned to invite the Chinese President Jiang Zemin to the United States in 1997 and then to visit China himself.

Jiang Zemin, too, desired to improve Sino–U.S. relations. That would consolidate his power in China and would strengthen China's position in the world. Perhaps his desire for better relations with Washington was stimulated by the Japan–U.S. joint declaration on security. On his way to the United States in October 1997, he first stopped in Honolulu and visited the Arizona Memorial at Pearl Harbor. In his speech there he reminded the American audience of the history of World War II, when China and the United States were allies. Because U.S.–China relations have been unfriendly most of the time since the birth of the People's Republic of China, it was natural for Jiang to evoke the memory of World War II so as to stress the friendship between the two nations in the past. But his visit to Pearl Harbor might have been an attempt to change the balance of America's East Asian policy, which seemed to have tilted toward Japan in the previous year. In a speech at the White House, President Clinton, too, recalled U.S.–Chinese cooperation and also referred specifically to Jiang's visit to Pearl Harbor. This Pearl Harbor symbolism certainly dismayed the Japanese diplomats in Washington.

It was also in 1997 that Iris Chang's *The Rape of Nanking: The Forgotten Holocaust of World War II* was published in the United States. This book, published in paperback form the following year, was widely read in the United States. The Japanese people should have known that one aspect of the post–Cold War era would be that people in the Western world began to reflect back beyond the Cold War years and to take more interest in scrutinizing crimes against humanity committed during World War II. The Japanese people will best be able to cope with this trend if they hold steadfastly the view of history that Prime Minister Murayama espoused in 1995 in his aforementioned statement on the 50th anniversary of the end of World War II. In this connection, it is regrettable that in recent years a group of Japanese intellectuals started a campaign to spread their self-righteously nationalistic view of modern Japanese history. Although they remain a small minority, they have already harmed Japan's credibility as a liberal democratic nation.

President Jiang's trip to the United States was a success. He gave many Americans the impression that he was a trustworthy leader who was well aware of the responsibility of China as a great power in the world. In June 1998, President Clinton made a return visit to China and stayed there for nine days, the same number of days that Jiang had spent in America. The Japanese news media noted the unusually long itinerary of the presidential visit. But what annoyed Japan's leaders was the seemingly contemptuous attitude toward Japan that Clinton exhibited in Beijing. When Jiang complained about the falling value of the Japanese yen, hinting that its decline was making it difficult for China to keep the value of its currency steady, Clinton agreed that Japan was quite a problem. He criticized Japan for deepening the economic difficulties of Asian countries by its mismanagement of its economy, and he praised China for its economic growth and for its efforts to keep the value of its currency steady so as to save Asia from further economic confusion. The U.S.

secretary of the treasury made similar comments in Beijing and in other Asian capitals concerning the economic performances of Japan and China.

Although it was true that the Hashimoto cabinet did not prevent the Japanese economy from falling into recession in 1997, U.S. criticism of Japan was not very fair, because Japan was the foremost country in supplying emergency assistance to Asian countries, such as Thailand, Indonesia, and Korea, in cooperation with the International Monetary Fund. There was a puzzlingly great gap between Clinton's praising Japan as an indispensable ally when he was in Tokyo in 1996 and his bashing Japan for its contemptible impotence during his visit to Beijing two years later. Why did he agree with China's economic views and dump Japan while in Beijing? It may be recalled that he and top Treasury Department officials had been criticizing Tokyo's inept economic policies since the previous year. The Clinton administration was afraid that if Japan's depressed economy delayed the economic recovery of Asian countries, it would disrupt the otherwise-thriving U.S. economy. Probably they wanted a scapegoat in case the prosperity of the U.S. economy was disturbed.

Just as Clinton gave Hashimoto a no-confidence vote from Beijing, so did the Japanese electorate in the upper-house election in July 1998. When the LDP lost a number of seats in that election, Hashimoto promptly resigned as prime minister and was succeeded by Keizō Obuchi, his foreign minister. Because Obuchi did not seem to be a particularly able man, he was referred to as "a cold pizza" by the international media. Ten years before, around the turn of the decade, Japanese people had assumed that the United States was a country in decline and made derogatory public remarks about Americans. It was now the turn for Americans to consider Japan passé and to make contemptuous remarks about the Japanese. So, very quickly, the two nations had traded places again. Meanwhile, subsequent developments in U.S.–China relations proved that their political partnership was not yet strong and would need many more years to mature. Euphoria about their partnership soon disappeared in both capitals. While U.S.–China relations deteriorated in 1999, the Clinton administration made several gestures to soothe Japan's wounded feelings. And because

Obuchi seemed to be doing better than expected, Washington treated him rather kindly when he visited Washington in May 1999.

*   *   *

The Japan–U.S. alliance has continued for 50 years, and it will continue well into the 21st century. During the past half-century, the Japan–U.S. relationship has been confronted by many problems, but the two nations, enemies in World War II, have managed to maintain their alliance in the midst of great changes in world politics and in the global economy. The Japan–U.S. alliance has been characterized by the asymmetrical nature of the two nations' respective roles: an alliance between the world's foremost military superpower and a country whose military role is restricted by its constitution. Both nations have accepted this basic character of the alliance and have maintained it with minor adjustments—to their mutual benefit. The remarkable resilience of the Japan–U.S. alliance, as stated in the joint Hashimoto–Clinton declaration of 1996, is fundamentally derived from the common values and interests that the two nations share. In retrospect, it can be said that Japan's defeat in World War II and the reform introduced during the U.S. occupation paved the way for the long-term friendship of the two nations by transforming Japan into a liberal, democratic nation. By developing a stable, liberal democracy and a viable economy, Japan was able to gain considerable international trust and respect in the second half of the 20th century. But the developments in 1998 taught the Japanese that Japan would not have much weight in the international community if the nation lost its economic viability. If a liberal and democratic Japan succeeds in regaining a viable economy, that success would enhance Japanese liberal democracy itself.

The Japanese people should make the 50th anniversary of the San Francisco Peace Treaty an occasion for appreciating how fortunate it was for Japan to be able to undergo drastic democratization after World War II and to return to the international community as a liberal democratic nation. Japan owes very much to the United States in this regard. This anniversary should also be a time for the Japanese people to reaffirm their commitment to liberal democratic values and to strive to strengthen their democratic tradition of 50 years by solving the nation's economic problems.

Chapter 2

THE AMERICANIZATION OF JAPANESE SOCIETY AND CULTURE

NAGAYO HONMA

Since World War II, Japanese society and culture have developed under the overwhelming influence of the United States of America. But the so-called Americanization of Japan didn't begin with Japan's defeat and occupation by U.S. forces. A glance at modern Japanese history will reveal that Japan has been subjected to American influence almost continuously since the Meiji Restoration, and that this influence has extended from religion and philosophy to everyday life.

In the pre-modern era Japan was deeply affected by China. In the Edo period, China was worshiped by Japanese scholars. According to a well-known anecdote, a noted Confucian philosopher named Ogyū Sorai was delighted when he moved from downtown Edo to Shinagawa, because it brought him a bit closer to China. In those days, to get an education meant to learn to read the Chinese classics. Children of *samurai* families were made to read *The Analects of Confucius* even if they didn't understand a word of it. Learned people composed Chinese poems—a tradition that was carried on into the Meiji era. Marius Jansen, the distinguished American scholar of modern Japanese history, once said that it is hard to find another example of a country in which a foreign culture and tradition have been so highly regarded. But that was because the Japanese in the Edo period never had a chance to see actual life in China. When direct contract with China became possible in the Meiji era, the idealized image of China was destroyed.

In contrast, the history of Japan's relation with America has been based on direct contact in two dimensions—exchanges of people and of goods—ever since Commodore Perry arrived in the mid-19th century. This might partly explain why the Japanese as a people have never completely idolized America, as Confucian scholars did China during the Edo Period. Rather, educated people of the Meiji era tended to be critical of American culture and traditions—a phenomenon that can still be observed today. As Shunsuke Kamei, an astute observer of American culture, pointed out, Japan's dealings with the United States have always been characterized by two opposing tendencies—America-worship and anti-Americanism. There are both those who happily accept the tendency toward Americanization, and those who see it as undesirable—and these two contradictory attitudes can even be observed in one person. Young intellectuals in the Meiji era had a longing for America and dreamed of going there. They eagerly sought out and listened to those who returned from visits to America. It is said that when Waseda University was founded, people talked enthusiastically of emulating Harvard or Yale. When American cultural influence rapidly spread around the world after World War I, Japan eagerly received it. In his 1929 book *America*, Takanobu Murofushi enthusiastically wrote as if the Americanization of Japan had already been completed: "Where is Japan that isn't American? Can Japan exist without America? Where can one still find a life that isn't American? I am sure of it. America is not only the world itself, but Japan today has become nothing other than America itself."

These words were, of course, an exaggeration. To be sure, there was a broad Americanization of popular culture in the form of movies, jazz music, baseball, and literature. But the same recording and radio-broadcasting technologies that popularized American music also made traditional Japanese chants available throughout the country. Thus, children in the 1930s listened to westernized songs like "Kohan no yado" (An inn on the lake) by Mieko Takamine on the radio, along with traditional Japanese stories like "The Legend of Shimizu Jirochō" by Torazō Hirosawa. There were certainly large parts of Japanese life that were left untouched by the wave of Americanization.

Even so, most of the foreign heroes familiar to the Japanese in those years were Americans. There was a period during the Meiji era when a song praising George Washington was popular among middle school students, and the tale of Washington's confession to his father that it was he who had chopped down the cherry tree has been known to every Japanese school child since that era. Abraham Lincoln, too, was the subject of numerous biographies written for young people, and so were Thomas A. Edison, the inventor; John D. Rockefeller, the oil king; Andrew Carnegie, the builder of the American steel industry; and John Wanamaker, the creator of the department store.

Given that history, the four years that followed Pearl Harbor should be seen as an aberration in the long course of Americanization of Japanese society and culture that began at the start of the Meiji era.

1. WORLD WAR II AND THE POSTWAR PERIOD

After Japan declared war against the United States, the Japanese were discouraged from learning about and enjoying enemy culture. American and English music and folk songs in high school textbooks were passed over and not taught. Terms used in baseball were replaced by Japanese words that sounded constrained. Nonetheless, there were high schools that continued to teach English through the war. Some students at Tokyo Imperial University even secretly organized a screening of *Gone with the Wind*.

One item of historical material that illustrates Japanese intellectuals' perceptions about their country's modernization during the war years is a collection of essays written in 1942 for the monthly *Bungakukai*, or *Literary World*. For its cover project in the September and October issues, the magazine collected essays by people in various fields, including writers, philosophers, historians, scientists, and film critics, concerning Western-style modernization and its effects, both positive and negative, on Japan. Author Fusao Hayashi, who was born in 1904 and had given up his leftist views, wrote that as a result of the modernization process he had gone through, he couldn't help laughing when he heard chants by Shinto priests. Because he had spent so much time learning English, Japanese classics like *The Tale of Heike* and *Tsurezure-gusa* seemed as through they were written in a foreign language.

Film critic Hideo Tsumura argued that Americanism is about making human life into something artificial and subjecting it to the magical power of automation. "I see no valuable element, nothing worthy of emulating, in Americanism," he wrote. On the other side of the spectrum, European history expert Shigetaka Suzuki offered the opinion that America's high standard of living represented both its strength and its weakness. Suzuki recognized not only materialism but also spiritualism in America, and he admired its high living standard—even during the war.

The world began to see America's unsurpassed influence on global politics, economy, military affairs, and culture only after the war ended, but some Americans were talking about the 20th century as their own time even before their country had entered the conflict. Henry Luce, the publisher of *Time, Life,* and *Fortune* magazines, wrote a long essay entitled "The American Century," which was published in the February 1941 issue of *Life.* It had such a major impact that it was later published as a book. In it, Luce argued that if the United States could get rid of its isolationist mindset, the 20th century would certainly be America's century, because jazz, Hollywood movies, American slang, and American machinery were already spreading across the world.

To realize the vision of the "American Century," Luce said that the United States should promote the dynamic development of free enterprise. Second, he said, the country needed to become a training center for technological development. Beyond that, Luce wanted America to be a Good Samaritan—to help those in need and to become a power station of freedom and justice. To Luce, those were the ideals for the 20th century, and Americans should be delighted to devote themselves to making the vision come true. Some of Luce's contemporaries embraced his vision and used it to promote peace and stability in the world. His argument about the "American Century" even spurred some debate in the House of Representatives. But there were also those who saw imperialist tendencies in the idea, including noted theologian Reinhold Niebhur, who worried about the arrogance implied in Luce's vision of the "American Century."

After World War II, scholars of international politics began to use the term *American Century* to mean world domination by the United States, backed by its military might. As the United States came to be recognized as a superpower, President Truman declared that the American Century had arrived, and expressed a hope that it would turn into a "human century" some day.

To advance the clock for a moment, the American influence in the world and its self-confidence as a model for democratic societies began to wane in the late 1960s, particularly after the U.S. defeat in the Vietnam War. In this regard, a book titled *The End of the American Era* was published in 1970, and some began to argue that the "American Century" had really lasted for only 20 years. More recently, a 1996 book, titled *The American Century* was subtitled *The Rise and Fall of America's Power*.

But in the late 1940s, it was an objective truth that the United States overshadowed all other nations—not only the vanquished, but also the victorious—with its economic and military might, and many American leaders saw that as the victory of American democracy. Just so, the purported goal of U.S. Occupation policy in Japan was to democratize the country through various reform programs, and to prevent a resurgence of militarism, so as to keep Japan from ever again becoming a threat to world peace. Among the various Occupation reform programs, the most notable in terms of its cultural effect was that concerning education. In January 1946, the Allied General Headquarters asked the U.S. Army to send American educators to Japan to advise and consult with the GHQ as well as with Japanese educators. The Army sent 27 experts, selected by the State Department, who arrived in Japan in early March and presented a report to General MacArthur on March 31.

In a 1979 analysis published along with a Japanese translation of the report, educator Minoru Murai said that it was "one of three documents that changed more than one hundred years of the history of education in Japan since the beginning of Meiji." (One of the other two, he said, was the Imperial Rescript on Education.) The report, Murai wrote, defined the direction of post-war reconstruction of Japanese education, which since then "has been moving along the ambit [it] laid out . . . , without regard to reality." In essence, the report, he argued, was the basic document for the Americanization of education in Japan.

The report was well-received by MacArthur, who called it a "document of high ideals, based on democratic traditions." The Japanese government set up a committee for the renewal of education and worked with the Education Ministry and the GHQ to implement policies based on the report. These included the Basic Law on Education, which provided for the system of six years of elementary school followed by three years of middle school, under the control of local boards of education.

Rereading the report today, it is clear that the American mission wasn't suggesting the implementation in Japan of an exact copy of the U.S. education system in form and substance. In its introduction, the report said, "We would not be happy to have our institutions superficially copied. We believe in the progress and evolution of society, and we welcome the diversity of cultures that covers the world as a source of hope and rejuvenating power." Clearly the group had respect for Japanese traditions and cultural resources, and it recommended that the educational system make use of them in spreading democracy in Japan. The notion that education can be a tool in making democracy truly take root in a society is based on John Dewey's educational philosophy, which was prevalent in the United States at the time.

It is no a simple matter to discuss how Japanese teachers reacted to the rapid Americanization of education during the Occupation. In regard to this, however, Nobuo Kojima's short novel *American School*, though it is a work of fiction, offers an interesting observation. In that book, the author gives a somewhat caricatured description of the complex reaction of Japanese teachers of English in Japanese middle schools who go to see an American school. Some are proud to speak English, while others are left feeling humiliated. One teacher who has difficulty speaking English sees others who can speak the language, complete with gestures, and thinks, "It is a shame to speak perfectly like a *gaijin* [foreigner], but it is also a shame to speak the language imperfectly." One day he tries to start a class by saying, "Good morning, everybody," but that causes "the blood to rush to his head and making him feel like he was falling down a cliff." He felt that he wasn't the same person when he was speaking in English, and he strongly resented that.

Today, as we debate the controversy over Yōichi Funabashi's suggestion that English be Japan's second official language, it is interesting to read about the aforementioned feelings of resistance to

Americanization even during the Occupation. It is also interesting to compare the phenomenon with trends in the Edo period, when intellectuals enthusiastically learned Chinese.

2. THE CULTURE OF DEMOCRACY

Japan's defeat in World War II prompted a rush of American culture into the country. Presenting itself as a symbol of democracy, American culture not only deeply affected everything from popular ways to academic and artistic works, but also brought profound changes in Japanese values, lifestyles, and social institutions. But as I mentioned earlier, Japan had been importing varied forms of American culture ever since the Meiji period. When cultural exchanges resumed after having been disrupted during the war, there was already a thick accumulation of resources to build on. But the speed of acceptance of American ways, especially in the realm of popular culture, was vastly accelerated after the war because of the two countries' relative positions. America with its overwhelming power, was full of self-confidence that the "American Century" had arrived, while Japan was a vanquished nation whose self-confidence had been shattered because everything its people had been taught to believe had been negated. On top of that, the country was placed under the Occupation of a foreign power for the first time in its long history.

We have observed the complex nature of the cultural implications of the English language in Japan, as depicted by Nobuo Kojima in his novel *American School*. On August 30, 1945, just two weeks after the end of the war, *Nichibei Kaiwa Techo*, the *Handbook of Japanese-American Conversation* was published; it rapidly sold 4 million copies, becoming Japan's first postwar best-seller. Even the term *best-seller*, wasn't used until the weekly *Shūkan Asahi* was launched in 1946. In the following year, NHK radio launched its "English Conversation" program, with Yuiichi Hirakawa as instructor, to an enthusiastic reception. The program's theme song, an old children's tune with verses that include "Come, come, everybody . . . ," evokes nostalgia to many Japanese who lived through those days.

In April 1946, professional baseball again began to be placed in Japan. The history of baseball in Japan actually goes back a long way. The topic appears in Sōseki Natsume's *I Am A Cat*, one of Japan's first modern novels, and Shiki Masaoka who found haiku poems, loved baseball. Japan's first professional baseball game was played in February 1936, and the baseball tournaments among Tokyo's Big-Six universities were major events in prewar Japan. But it was after the war that professional baseball attained the status of a national pastime. The different ways in which the game is played and enjoyed in the two countries has been analyzed to gain insight into the differences in national character. Toward the end of the 20th century, several Japanese players signed up with major league teams in the United States, and one even was named Rookie of the Year. In the field of popular music, jazz became popular again, and boogie-woogie, unknown to Japan until after the war, got off to an explosive start in 1948, helped by the dynamic duo of composer Ryōichi Hattori and singer Shizuko Kasagi. It reached its peak in 1950 with the hit of "Shopping Boogie," a unique combination of Osaka dialect sung to a fast American beat, the idea for which was said to have been taken from the Japanese comic story-telling art of *rakugo*. The song's ending with "Gosh, I'm exhausted" in the amusing Osaka dialect exemplifies the fact that boogie-woogie was fully assimilated by Japanese culture.

In 1951, the Hattori–Kasagi team came up with a comical non-boogie song, called "Shopping in Los Angeles," about a girl who travels to the United States for the first time in her life. She struggles with her halting English to talk to a handsome soldier, who happens to have spent more than two years in Japan and speaks Japanese fluently. She buys a lot of cheap souvenirs to take back home, but they all turn out to have been made in Japan. And the refrain of the song is, "America's a nice place, I love America." Other popular songs of this period include "Longing for a Voyage to Hawaii," and "San Francisco Chinatown," indicating the growing desire of the Japanese public to visit Hawaii and the West Coast.

But it was also around this time that Japanese-style ballads known as *enka* became very popular. Two of the most popular singers at the time were Chiemi Eri whose debut song was "The Tennessee Waltz," and Hibari Misora who perfected a melange of *enka* and traditional folk songs in "Ringo Oiwake," or "The Apple-Packing Song," symbolizing the way in which American-style popular songs existed side by side with *enka*. The fact that the two singers criss-crossed each other's genre is also evidence of the assimilation of American culture in Japan.

Beginning around 1950, American hit songs were imported into Japan and became instant hits. Harry Belafonte, who became famous with his "Banana Boat Song," visited Japan several times, and he even began singing "Sakura Sakura" as part of his standard repertoire. Elvis Presley, known as "The King," never visited Japan, but enthusiastic Japanese fans organized fan clubs, complete with regular publications, and Graceland became a must-visit destination for Japanese worshippers. Elvis, along with Marilyn Monroe and John F. Kennedy, remain in the collective memories of the Japanese as American cultural icons even today.

As Takanobu Murofushi noted, in the prewar era the Japanese also acquired images of American life from Hollywood movies, another symbol of American culture in Japan. In 1948, the Subaru-za opened in Yūrakuchō, downtown Tokyo, becoming Japan's first theater to specialize in American movies, showing *American Symphony*, a story of George Gershwin, as its first feature. A few years later, *Gone With the Wind* hit the screen in Japan with great fanfare, in what would be the first of several visits to the theater in the years that followed. Many Japanese regarded Scarlett O'Hara as an example of the strong-minded women of America, while others compared the South under Union control to Japan under the U.S. Occupation.

Movies that might damage the image of America as an affluent society, such as *The Grapes of Wrath* and *Tobacco Road* were not shown in Japan during the Occupation. Film-noir movies that portrayed the dark sides of American society and human feelings, many of them produced during and immediately after the war, weren't imported until after 1952. Although Westerns and gangster movies were considered typical American fare, the Japanese movie-going public also became familiar with features depicting the moods and interests of American society throughout the postwar period. Lately, the technology of special effects also has been of great interest to the Japanese.

In prewar Japan, American movies were considered mere entertainment, and not valuable works of art, and this view persisted after the war, especially among intellectuals. But as movies became a subject of academic research, directors like Alfred Hitchcock and Howard Hawks came to be appreciated for their craftsmanship in making highly sophisticated entertainment. Some argue that American influence was evident in the works of Yasujirō Ozu and Akira Kurosawa, who won international acclaim with their depiction of universal human messages in settings that seemed exclusively Japanese.

Broadway musicals, which had their heyday from the late 1940s through the end of the 1960s, reached Japan with some time lag. The first major Japanese production of a musical was that of *Gone With the Wind*, adapted by Kazuo Kikuta and staged by the Takarazuka Girls' Review in 1966. It was followed by Japanese versions of Broadway musicals, such as *The Man of La Mancha* featuring Kōshirō Matsumoto and *The Fiddler on the Roof* with Hisaya Morishige. Their great successes—each was performed more than 900 times—helped make American-style musicals a staple of the Japanese entertainment industry.

In the field of art, American works attracted little attention in Japan before the war. But postwar artists, such as Jackson Pollack of "action painting" fame, socially-conscious Ben Shahn, Edward Hopper, who depicted American scenes, and Andy Worhol, the king of pop-art became very popular in Japan. Their works are often on exhibit, and they have become the subjects of serious study by Japanese academics and researchers.

Modern American music didn't win as large a following in Japan as American art did. Music by "Sunday composer" Charles Ives, which became very popular in post-war America, was not appreciated in Japan as much as were works by John Cage. But in the United States, the internationalization of the American musical scene, which began with an influx of European artists before and during World War II, continued with the participation of Japanese musicians. Most notable was the Boston Symphony's appointment of Seiji Ozawa as its conductor, but he was followed by many talented Japanese instrumental musicians who studied at the Juilliard School and ascended to fame thereafter.

In academic research, Japan's effort to make up for the blank space created by the war was greatly helped by the Fulbright Program, which funded scholarly exchanges. Many Japanese scholars and students were given chances to learn about the latest developments in natural and social science at American institutions. For a while after the war, Marxist economic theory was in vogue in Japanese universities, which used it to analyze the Japanese economy and to make policy proposals. But as Paul Samuelson's modern economic theory became the main-stream in the United States, it became widely accepted in Japan as well. Samuelson's basic economics textbook has long been the standard in Japanese universities. In relatively new academic fields, such as cultural anthropology, international relations, community development, social psychology and business management, Japan has been greatly affected by developments in the United States.

Many Japanese who obtained M.B.A.s in American universities have gone on to take senior executive positions in Japanese corporations. American influence is evident in the intellectual scenery of postwar Japan. The fact that the works of Alexis de Tocqueville were suddenly dusted off and opened up is a reflection of the reevaluation of the 19th century French philosopher in the United States, especially after David Riesman quoted him in *The Lonely Crowd*. Riesman visited Japan in 1962 at the invitation of the International House of Japan to partic-ipate in its intellectual-exchange program. Although he wasn't a researcher on Japan, he vigorously engaged in activities to observe Japan and to exchange opinions with Japanese interested in his work.

Rachel Carson was another American author who influenced Japan's priorities. Japan was slow to react to her *Silent Spring*, first published in the *New Yorker* magazine. But as environmental pollu-tion worsened, concerned Japanese turned to her writings, and the word *ecology* became a part of Japanese vocabulary. America also made an impact on Japan in the area of sexual equality. Inspired by Betty Friedan's *The Feminine Mystique* and by formation of the National Organization for Women, which she chaired, "*ūman ribu*" as women's liberation is called in Japan made a debut in Japan in 1970 with this nation's first symposium, held in Tokyo on the subject. Creation in the U.S. of new academic disciplines such as feminine his-tory, women's studies and gender analysis, were also repeated in Japan with some time lag. Although the Equal Rights Amendment to the U.S. Constitution was never ratified, Japan's Diet was able to pass an equal employment opportunity law in 1985, and various efforts to end gender discrimination are under way in the government as well as in the private sector.

Looking back at the end of the 20th century, it is clear that priorities in social science research have changed a great deal since the years immediately after World War II. Words like *ecology, gender, multiculturalism,* and *ethnicity* have become much more important. Also, the advent of the Internet has made startling changes in how research is conducted. Not all of these changes can be attributed to Americanization: One must consider that European scholars, writers, and critics also have made considerable impact. There were developments resulting from indigenous research in Japan as well. Even so, there is no denying that the magnitude of American influence in academic research was much greater in postwar Japan than it was in the pre-war era.

After the war, a number of distinguished scholars of Japanese studies, including Edwin Reischauer and Marius Jansen, emerged in the United States. These scholars, who were also well known in Japan, not only took the lead in nurturing the next generation of scholars in the United States, but also engaged themselves in lively discussions with Japanese researchers on subjects such as modernization during the Meiji period. That established the precedent for the many joint-research projects between American and Japanese scholars that followed, on subjects ranging from Japanese history and U.S.–Japan relations to general international relations.

In prewar Japan, academic studies of America were limited to lectures by Professor Yasaka Takagi of Tokyo Imperial University. After the war, various academic organizations, including The Japanese Association for American Studies (JAAS) and the American Literature Association of Japan, were formed. A variety of research projects were organized, and many researchers made use of original materials to come up with interesting findings. Today, membership in the Society of American Studies exceeds 1,000.

Japanese society has gone through a radical transformation since the end of World War II, and it no longer seems valid to apply the term "postwar" to Japan. Starting from the period of chaos immediately after the war, the material wealth of the Japanese increased steadily through the reconstruction period, and then through the high-growth era. The Japanese standard of living—in itself a very American concept—has risen continuously. Hollywood movies, American magazines and comic strips like "Blondie!," spread the image of an "American lifestyle." Since the mid 1950s, refrigerators, washing machines and vacuum cleaners have been the "three sacred treasures" in every Japanese home, and by the end of that decade, vacuum cleaners were followed on the new "treasure" list by television sets. The early days of Japanese television broadcasts were filled mostly with American programs accompanied by Japanese voice-over soundtracks. Toward the end of the century, personal computers began to invade Japanese homes as well as offices, prompting politicians to speak of an information-technology revolution, or "IT revolution."

Americanization is often symbolized by Coca-Cola, which prompted someone to coin the term "Coca-colonization." The Atlanta-based maker of the popular soft drink set up a Japanese subsidiary in 1957, as it expanded operations around the globe. Next came the McDonald's hamburger, which has become a synonym for fast food. It was not until 1971 that McDonald's opened its first restaurant in Japan, in Ginza, but in less than eight years the company was ringing up more than ¥100 billion a year in sales. In the late 1990s, Starbucks coffee shop followed in the footsteps of McDonald's. By then, chain family restaurants were all over Japan, and convenience stores and supermarkets had long ago replaced the old-fashioned mom-and-pop stores and were playing essential roles in the lives of Japanese consumers. The Americanization of Japanese street scenes had reached a point at which old jokes like the one about the child who went to Hawaii and said, "Mommy, there's McDonald's in Hawaii, too," were no longer funny.

In 1970, the Japan National Railway, the predecessor of the Japan Railway (JR) Companies, launched a tourism campaign called "Discover Japan," which turned out to be very effective, especially with young women. Its success was due at least partly to the fact that it captured a lingering nostalgia for scenes that are uniquely Japanese, but that are disappearing rapidly after years of Americanization, especially in big cities like Tokyo.

As Japanese living standards rose, one business that benefited enormously was the leisure industry, which cannot be discussed without mentioning Walt Disney and Disneyland. Disney cartoons were around in prewar Japan, but their popularity really took off after the war, particularly with the release of animation films like *Snow White* and *101 Dalmatians*, and musicals such as *Mary Poppins* that had good special effects. But the event that stands out in the development of the leisure industry in Japan is the opening of Tokyo Disneyland in 1982. People could now go to see Mickey Mouse at any time, and children as well as grownups, Japanese as well as foreign visitors, flocked to spend time at its bayside location in Chiba Prefecture. Now Disney characters are all over Japan, as stuffed animals, on school supplies, and on clothes and dishes. One could call this the "Disneyfication" of the Japanese leisure industry. The other American comic characters that have always been popular in Japan are Charlie Brown and his lovable dog Snoopy. Just as they continue to appear in American newspapers even after the death of their creator, Charles Schultz, Snoopy and his friends are immortalized in a multitude of commercial goods and posters in Japan. In terms of their contribution to the Americanization of the Japanese consumer culture, however, Charlie Brown and Snoopy can't begin to compete with Mickey and Company.

3. JAPAN–U.S. CULTURAL EXCHANGES

The United States wielded enormous influence around the world after the war, and its relationship with Japan was a lopsided one— the winner vs. the loser, the occupier vs. the occupied, the most affluent country in the world versus a country trying to catch up. Given the relative positions of the two countries, it was natural that most of the people and materials involved in bilateral cultural exchanges flowed west from the United States to Japan. But by the end of the 20th century, Japan was making contributions in various fields.

Among organizations whose aim is to promote understanding between the United States and Japan through cultural exchanges, some, like the America–Japan Society, Inc., have existed since before the war. After the war, the International House of Japan was created, thanks to the efforts of Shigeharu Matsumoto, as a vehicle for the exchange of intellectual ideas on higher levels. In the early 1960s, Prime Minister Hayato Ikeda and President John F. Kennedy agreed to establish the U.S.–Japan Conference on Cultural and Educational Interchange. It provided a venue for government and private-sector experts from the two countries to discuss ways to promote mutual understanding in educational and cultural fields.The Center for Global Partnership, set up under the Japan Foundation, has been providing financial assistance to various exchange programs at both the intellectual and the grass-roots levels.

The America–Japan Societies in Japan and in the United States have been working both individually and in cooperation with one another to plan and execute a variety of exchange programs to promote friendship. Some of the America–Japan Societies have also worked effectively with universities and academic groups to carry out intellectual exchange programs.

The question is whether these and other exchange programs in the half-century since the end of the war have truly deepened understanding between our countries. There is also a question of how to measure the degree of mutual understanding between the two countries. Conducting periodic opinion polls and surveys, and tracing changes in the numbers is one way. But that doesn't provide a clear answer to the question.

It is not hard to find statistics that show the imbalance in U.S.–Japan cultural exchanges. It is well known that American students studying in Japan are vastly outnumbered by Japanese students in American institutions of learning. Various efforts, including the creation of short-term study programs, are beeing made to correct the imbalance. But the gist of the problem is how to whet the appetites of American students to come to Japan to study.

A similar imbalance exists in the publishing industry. American books that attract attention in the United States, whether they are fiction, nonfiction, or scholarly works, are almost always translated into Japanese, regardless of their length. In contrast, only a small number of Japanese books are published in English through commercial channels. Even with a considerable amount of effort through other channels, very few Japanese books, particularly academic works, become available in English—and those that do are usually read by no more than a handful of experts. Still, the products of Japanese culture are abundantly visible in the United States, even if the people who use them don't realize that they originated in Japan. As Japanese exports to the United States grew and became increasingly sophisticated after the 1960s, the old image of Japanese products as cheap and shoddy disappeared. In a recent survey conducted in the Tokyo area, instant *ramen* noodles were picked as Japan's greatest single cultural contribution to the world—followed by *karaoke* and portable head-phone stereo systems.

Traditional Japanese art has come to be appreciated by overseas audiences, thanks partly to programs sponsored by the Japan Foundation to introduce such forms as *noh, kabuki, ikebana*, the tea ceremony, and *taiko* drums. Most popular among traditional Japanese art forms might be *haiku*, which has spread not only in the U.S. but throughout the world. Many American schools encourage students to compose *haiku*-style short English poems. Unfortunately, it is hard to assert that an appreciation of traditional Japanese arts necessarily contributes to a deeper understanding of contemporary Japanese culture and society.

For the last 50 years, Japanese society has been affected enormously by American culture. The extent of this historical process can be called "Americanization" in general. It also produced "Coca-colonization," "Disneyfication," "McDonaldization," and more recently, "Microsoftization," in their respective fields. Opinions are divided about whether all this is just the Americanization of consumer culture. It is well known that Tokyo Disneyland was a great success from the moment of its opening. Now we are told that Euro Disneyland in France has also seen an increase in visitors from 9.7 million in 1993 to 12.7 million in 1997. It might be appropriate to say that American culture, or at least mass culture, has spread around the world to become a "second culture" in many countries.

However, each country has had a unique process by which it integrated American culture into its own. In the case of Japan, there was also a process of "Japanization" of American culture along with the Americanization of Japanese culture. That explains the fact that Japanese culture remains distinctly Japanese in spite of the torrential influx of the American culture to which Japan has been exposed in the 50 years since the end of the war. That is also why Samuel Huntington, in his *Clash of Civilizations*, divided the contemporary world into nine civilizations, but treated Japan as a distinctly independent civilization. He even said that if economic integration is based on cultural commonality, Japan could be in for a very lonely economic future.

Huntington also discussed the universality of what he called the "Davos culture" in his book. People who gather at the annual World Economic Forum in the Swiss resort at Davos are generally highly educated, have international perspectives, travel abroad frequently, speak English fluently, and believe in individualism, market economics and democratic political systems, he said. But the number of people who share the Davos culture is minuscule as a percentage of the world population.

The Huntington theory stirred controversy in both the United States and Japan, but mainly over his argument that a clash of civilizations will be the fundamental cause of wars in the world to come. In discussing cultural relations between the United States and Japan, one can say that Japan's inner identity hasn't changed at all, because American cultural influence has been limited to the realm of consumption activities. The life of a consumer is profoundly related to his or her values. How an individual decides to spend time and money in everyday life depends on those values, which have been formed by assimilating basic American values like freedom, equality, individualism, and the pursuit of happiness.

Those who are tied to each other through the Davos culture will continue to share common values and lifestyles that transcend national borders. Quite apart from these members of the international elite, vast numbers of people, mainly in the younger generation, are developing a cultural solidarity through music and other expressions of popular culture. In that sense, the transmitter of democratic culture has been the United States in the last half of the 20th century, and it will continue to be so for sometime to come.

In developing its relationship with the United States in this new century, Japan should become more autonomous, while at the same time continuing to learn from history and building on common accomplishments achieved in the last half-century. The challenge to future generations of Japanese and Americans is to maintain their cultural differences but for both peoples to polish their respective culture to make it more attractive to the other. It will be good if we can build on a mutual understanding of our cultural commonality while continuing to be actively curious about each other's culture.

Chapter 3

GAINING FOOTHOLDS IN U.S. MARKETS:
Japanese Manufacturers and Their Management Practices

Immediately after World War II, when Japan was struggling to rebuild its war-torn economy with U.S. assistance, no one predicted that such a large number of Japanese companies would successfully make inroads into U.S. markets in the near future.

Throughout the 1950s and early 1960s, Japanese companies that would become locomotives of the postwar recovery of the domestic economy in later years were still desperately learning American business-management techniques, particularly quality control and systematic business administration. Japanese industrial products were poor and uneven in quality, and were far inferior to their American counterparts, which were manufactured under quantified quality-control systems.

Japanese manufacturers, without exception, hardly imagined they would ever be able to catch up with American companies in productivity, product quality, and technologies. A sense of resignation prevailed both in the Japanese government and in the private sector. Their modest hope was that such a resource-poor, small country as Japan could live on international trade following in the footsteps of the United States. No one imagined that Japanese industries and companies would overpower their American counterparts, cause trade frictions with the United States and start production in that country.

Two "lucky" factors helped Japanese industries and companies emerge from the rock-bottom position that they occupied in the period immediately after the war.

One factor was that Japan was woven into a free-trade system under the GATT that was initiated by the United States. Japan fully enjoyed the benefits of free trade. The other factor was that the United States adopted a foreign policy designed to turn Japan into a reliable ally in Asia. It supported Japan's economic recovery and development.

Japanese industries and companies, for their part, also made self-help efforts, learning what they should learn from the United States. The United States, in addition to providing economic assistance, also provided Japan with a variety of business techniques to modernize old-fashioned Japanese industries, including personnel-management and budget-control systems, and to enable Japanese companies to gain international competitive edges.

Japanese companies acquired U.S. management techniques quickly, adapting them to Japanese corporate culture. Such efforts resulted in the establishment of so-called Japanese-style management.

The increased competitive edge of Japanese products and the resulting increase of Japanese exports to United States caused a series of political issues between the two countries. Starting with a skirmish over the Japanese export of textiles in 1970, exports of steel, home appliances, electronics, automobiles, and semiconductors caused problems for American industries one after another.

Behind a series of Japan–U.S. trade frictions was the overall decline of the U.S. economy due to huge budget deficits caused partly by the Vietnam War. Major U.S. companies began to decline and to lose their international competitiveness. The quality of American industrial products consequently deteriorated. U.S. companies' ability to develop products also declined, and management-labor relations became unstable and worsened. In other words, U.S. companies in those days failed to live up to the basic principles of modern business management, including quality control and marketing, that they had once taught to the Japanese.

A sharp increase in the global competitiveness of Japanese industries and the decline of U.S. major industries' global competitiveness took place concurrently, causing trade friction between the two countries throughout the 1970s and 1980s. The high point came in 1981, when a dispute flared over Japanese automobile imports. The problem was temporarily solved by voluntary curbs on car exports to the United States, but the final solution was local production in the United States by Japanese automotive manufacturers.

Japanese electric and electronics companies had already started production in the United States in the 1970s, when they started assembling electric appliances in their newly built U.S. plants in an effort to reduce their exports to the United States from Japan. That move was followed by similar actions by many other Japanese manufacturers.

The rush of Japanese manufacturers to North America reached a climax when Japanese auto makers finally decided to build their cars in the United States.

As the number of Japanese manufacturers operating in the United States increased, Japanese production techniques, including Toyota's "just-in-time" manufacturing system, were adopted by U.S. manufacturers. This had a great impact on U.S. industries that had been suffering from a decline of competitiveness, and it contributed to their revival.

Throughout the 1980s, U.S. manufacturers learned a lot from their Japanese counterparts, and they are still learning. With the start of globalization, however, the United States again began taking the lead, particularly in the banking and securities sectors of the world, because the United States has been effectively utilizing information technology.

With such an overview of the post-war economic/business relations between Japan and the United States as the background, this paper clarifies how Japanese companies started doing business in the U.S. market and how they then started local manufacturing there. It also shows how Japanese-style production techniques, particularly those of Japanese automobile companies, contributed to the revival of their American counterparts. In addition, it proposes what Japanese industries should learn from their U.S. counterparts, which made an astonishing comeback by learning from

the Japanese. Last, this paper also clarifies the historical significance, in regard to Japan–U.S. economic relations, of Japanese
manufacturers producing in the United States.

1. JAPANESE MANUFACTURERS MAKING INROADS INTO U.S.
MARKETS, AND THE BACKGROUND THEREOF

Initially, there were two different reasons for Japanese manufacturers to start production in the United States.

One group of manufacturers, with no trade problems with U.S.
companies, ventured into the United States because they saw a great
potential for their business in the huge North American market.
The major cause that drove another group of Japanese manufacturers to local production there was trade friction. They started
assembling their products in North America in an effort to maintain their presence in that market, a presence that they had
painstakingly developed by their exports from Japan.

Kikkoman, a leading Japanese soy sauce manufacturer that built
a plant in Wisconsin, was among the first group of companies. TV
manufacturers, including Matsushita Electric Industrial, which
bought a plant in Chicago from Motorola, was among the second
group. Coincidently, both Kikkoman and Matsushita Electric started production in the United States in 1972.

Building a manufacturing plant in the United States was part of
the marketing strategy of Kikkoman, a producer of the Japanese
traditional seasoning of soy sauce. The demand for soy sauce was
expected to increase in the North American market.

In those days, two major ingredients of soy sauce—soy beans
and wheat—were imported from Midwest U.S. states to Japan. The
soy sauce manufacturer assumed that by making soy sauce in the
U.S. it could save the cost of importing materials and could quickly meet the growing local demand. Kikkoman built a plant in
Walworth, Wisconsin, where the traditional soy-sauce brewery
process was modernized and automated with biochemical technology. Also, labor-saving equipment was introduced, offsetting the
high cost of labor in the United States.

Kikkoman's success of local production owed much to its consistent marketing policy: creating new demand by slightly changing Americans' eating habits.

In the United States, the Chinese had been making Chinese-style, thick soy sauce that was sold mostly to Chinese restaurants. However, unlike Chinese soy sauce, the Japanese sauce is rather plain, because wheat is added to the soy beans during the manufacturing process. Kikkoman thought that Japanese soy sauce could be adapted for use with many American dishes, including beef steak, that in general lack delicate taste.

With this belief, which later was proven correct, Kikkoman kicked off campaigns to create a soy sauce market in the United States by its own power. In addition to traditional Japanese soy sauce, it developed a new barbecue sauce by adding wine to soy sauce for the U.S. market.

In the late 1960s, interest in Japanese-style meals was growing in America. At about that same time, many U.S. servicemen returned home after having had sukiyaki and other Japanese dishes while stationed in Japan. The demand for soy sauce was about to skyrocket in the United States.

Under such circumstances, Kikkoman moved to start production in Wisconsin. Actually, local production further expanded the soy-sauce and barbecue-sauce markets quickly. Most American steak houses began to use soy sauce and barbecue sauce. Moreover, these products became regular items at supermarkets across the United States.

As mentioned earlier, the motive of Japanese home appliance manufacturers for building assembly plants in the United States during the 1970s was the different from Kikkoman's. What drove them to local production was the difficulty of keeping up exports from Japan, mainly because of the change of the currency-exchange system and intensified disputes over the companies' exports to the United States. The fixed currency-exchange-rate system was caused to shift to a floating-rate system by U.S. President Richard Nixon in 1971, when he declared that the United States would no longer exchange U.S. dollars for gold.

Two manufacturers took the lead in starting local production in the United States: Sony and Matsushita Electric Industrial. In 1972,

Sony built an assembly plant for color television sets in San Diego, California. Soon it added a plant for manufacturing cathode-ray tubes (CRTs), the main component of a television set, and increased its production of color TVs.

Unlike Sony, which built brand-new manufacturing plants, Matsushita bought an existing color-TV plant in Chicago from Motorola in 1974. Matsushita took over not only the plant and equipment, but also the plant's management and employees as well as its brand, Quasar.

At Matsushita Quasar, Matsushita's new company for producing TV sets in the United States, the Japanese way of management was introduced immediately. At the beginning of work every morning, short meetings were held at the workshop, enhancing communications between management and employees. Human contacts were given more attention in personnel management. Work evaluations were done not only by paper, but also by other means. Also, recreation and the welfare of employees were considered very important. In assigning, promoting, and training employees, human factors and enhancing the capacities of employees were fully taken into account. Horizontal communications among workers were encouraged, and awareness of teamwork was raised. As a result, employee turnover declined and absenteeism decreased.

In 1978, the American president of Matsushita Quasar told me about the Matsushita way of management. He did not seem to think that the Japanese way of management was very peculiar, saying that coordination and harmonization among organizational functions, emphasis on mutual trust, and quick response to problems and feedback in Matsushita's management are business principles that every company should seek to apply. He added, however, that it is necessary to pay attention to different responses when those principles are applied to people of different cultural backgrounds.

Although the Japanese-style management was introduced at Matsushita Quasar, an American-style system was partially maintained in the company's production system. Two kinds of assembly lines, American and Japanese, were operated in parallel to make TV circuits. In the American-style assembly lines that Matsushita inherited from Motorola, each worker was required to do just a single task. Every worker did a different task, and he or she was responsible for no more than that. In the Matsushita-style assembly line, every worker was responsible for several tasks. In the American-style assembly line there were TV monitors that automatically checked the quality of the circuit boards that had been assembled. Matsushita officials said, however, that this American monitoring system helped them, to a certain extent, to increase production in the United States.

The Matsushita management found that the American assembly system was premised on two factors: the clarification of the responsibility of individual workers employed by contract, and the use of workers who were capable of doing only one simple task. Because workers represented more than 20 ethnic groups and nationalities, and because some could not even speak English, Matsushita had to take into account the philosophy of the American assembly system.

Matsushita had to operate on the premises of the American system in organizing and implementing its management system and assembly lines. This actually helped Matsushita to develop system technologies for effective and efficient production utilizing workers having only single duties.

However, the American system had some shortcomings. It lacked coordination among the workers. It failed to develop workers' sense of loyalty to the company. It failed to upgrade the capacity of workers, because they engaged in only simple work, and it did not promote workers' sense of fulfillment.

Fortunately, the Japanese way of management happened to make up for those shortcomings. The Matsushita Quasar plant was the first to blend American and Japanese management systems.

Following Sony and Matsushita, Japanese home-appliance manufacturers, including Hitachi, Toshiba, Sharp, and Sanyo, also built plants in the United States to produce mainly color television sets.

While the Japanese electronics manufacturers expanded their production in the United States, American home-appliance manufacturers, including General Electric (GE), Westinghouse, Motorola, and Zenith moved their production bases abroad, mainly to Southeast Asian countries and Mexico. During this period, the "hollowing out" of the U.S. home-appliances industry took place.

Eventually, Japanese electronic manufacturers supplied their products to their U.S. counterparts under OEM agreements. For instance, Sharp produced Sears-brand color television sets and Hitachi provided large-size TV sets to GE. It is noteworthy that Motorola quickly pulled out of television manufacturing and concentrated its investment and management resources on the semiconductor business that had been regarded as an electronics business of the future. With the adoption of NAFTA, Japanese electronics makers began to move their color-television production to Mexico, where labor costs were lower. Matsushita Quasar was among such TV manufacturers, and it is still manufacturing TV sets in Mexico.

2. LATE STARTERS: JAPANESE AUTOMOBILE MAKERS AND AUTO COMPONENTS MAKERS

Some 10 years after electronics manufacturers began to assemble their products in the United States, Japanese automobile makers and auto-component manufacturers also began to assemble cars there in the 1980s. There are at least three reasons why auto manufacturers had to start local assembling in the United States later than electronics companies did.

First, Japanese electronics manufacturers quickly caught up with their American counterparts in terms of technology and gained international competitive edges by the 1970s. In contrast, Japanese automobile companies took more time to become internationally competitive than electronics companies did.

Second, it cost much more for an automobile company to build a plant than for an electronics firm to do so. The investment risk was far greater for automobile manufacturers than for electronics firms.

Third, Japanese auto companies found it difficult to find reliable local suppliers of components for their subcompact and compact cars. American parts companies were mainly producing components for larger-size cars. Consequently, when moving into the United States, Japanese auto manufacturers had to bring suppliers of small-car components with them. This made it more difficult for them to build cars in the United States.

The Japanese automobile industry had kept growing, relying on the domestic market, until 1973, when the first oil crisis hit Japan. Domestic demand for cars had greatly expanded throughout the 1960s, but the oil crisis halted the growth of domestic demand, forcing manufacturers to reduce production.

While domestic demand shrank, exports to the United States began to increase around 1974, partly because the oil crisis directed American consumers' attention to fuel-efficient small cars. The compact and subcompact car markets in the United States had been dominated by Europeans, including Volkswagen, but it was at about this time that Japanese cars became more popular than European ones, winning a reputation for their high-quality, fuel-efficiency, and low-cost.

What made the Japanese car industry sharply increase its international competitiveness? A study of the worldwide car industry by professors of the Massachusetts Institute of Technology revealed the reasons.

First, the Japanese car companies, including Toyota Motor Corp., implemented "lean manufacturing." This production system is represented by Toyota's *kanban hōshiki* method or "just-in-time" production system. This system made it possible to minimize the inventory of components, the waste of materials, mishandling, and defects at assembly lines. It also made it possible to flexibly change production lines for improvement when problems occurred and to upgrade product quality by organizing "QC circles." This system challenged an established theory of American-style mass production that said that productivity and quality were trade-offs. Under the lean production system, it was possible simultaneously to improve both productivity and quality.

Another feature of the lean production system was the long-term, stable relationship between a manufacturer and its components suppliers. Under the *keiretsu* system of interlocking companies, car manufacturers and parts makers collaborated with each other. Suppliers guaranteed the quality of their products and strictly observed the specified delivery dates. Automobile companies gave technological support to their suppliers. Setting mid- to long-term targets, the companies involved jointly made efforts to streamline their operations and to reduce costs. Suppliers were involved in the early stage of new-car development, including designing.

Although relations between car companies and suppliers were long-term and stable, that did not mean that competition was excluded among suppliers within a *keiretsu*. Manufacturers occasionally ordered the same components from several suppliers, encouraging competition among them. Consequently, component suppliers were able to sharpen their competitive edges.

The product-development systems of Japanese car companies constituted the third feature of the production system that contributed to the increase of their competitiveness. Under these systems, cross-functional collaboration was promoted among departments involved in car designing, and several projects to develop new cars were conducted simultaneously. Suppliers were also involved in new-car development from an early stage. Also, chief officers in charge of product development were given great authority to oversee the entire operation of creating new cars. This system shortened the period of new-car development and reduced development costs.

The lean production system, under which product development, production, and component-supply systems functioned efficiently, proved to be effective in the 1970s and remained so throughout the 1980s.

The second oil crisis, which was triggered by political turmoil in Iran at the end of 1978, doubled gas prices in the United States. American cars, dubbed gas guzzlers, faced a serious problem.

Within two years after the second oil crisis, consumers radically shifted to compact and subcompact cars. The demand for compacts and subcompacts jumped from 40 percent of the total car market to 60 percent. The "Big Three" had to revise their product strategies to produce more small cars. That change of strategies, however, forced them to spend huge amounts of money. As a result, U.S. auto industry was gripped by a serious recession. In 1981, Chrysler faced bankruptcy and was bailed out by the government. General Motors and Ford also slipped, experiencing severe deficits.

While Detroit was struggling with the recession, and while hundreds of thousands of auto workers lost their jobs, Japanese cars increased their market shares, intensifying the friction over Japanese car imports. The Japanese government had no other policy alternatives than to curb car exports to the United States, which appeared to be ever increasing. More than two million Japanese cars were being shipped to the United States annually. In May 1981, the Ministry of International Trade and Industry suggested that the Japanese car industry voluntarily set an annual export quota of 1.67 million units. By asking Japanese car makers to reduce their exports to the United States, the Japanese government tried to give the Big Three time to rehabilitate themselves and to solve the unemployment problem in the U.S. auto industry.

Facing such export quotas, executives of the Japanese automotive companies had to decide if they would continue to export under government control or would build cars in the United States.

Action was first taken by Honda, which had been building motorcycles at its Marysville plant in Ohio since 1979. Honda added sedans to its U.S. assembly lines in 1982. Nissan immediately followed suit in 1983, assembling cars at Sumner, Tennessee. Toyota, jointly with GM, established New United Motor Manufacturing Inc. (NUMMI) in Fremont, California. In 1987, Mazda moved into Flat Rock, Michigan. In 1988, Toyota built its own manufacturing facility in Georgetown, Kentucky, and Mitsubishi, collaborating with Chrysler, started in Bloomington, Illinois. In 1989, Suzuki moved into Ontario, Canada, for joint car production, and Isuzu and Fuji jointly engaged in production in Lafayette, Indiana. Moreover, Honda and Toyota also started producing cars in Ontario, while Nissan built a plant in Mexico.

In the 1980s, almost all Japanese car manufacturers jumped on the wagon. A total of 13 plants of Japanese automobile companies are now operating in North America. Following in the footsteps of car manufacturers, Japanese components manufacturers also moved into the United States and built plants there. Their number has totaled more than 200. Some of them were so successful that they began to supply their products to the Big Three, too.

Initially, Japanese car makers were very careful in their ventures in the United States. They had to take into account both risks accompanying large investments amounting to ¥50 billion to ¥100 billion, and possible troubles with labor unions caused

by the differences of labor practices and different component-
supply systems. But trade friction with the U.S. became so intensified, and electronics companies were so successful in local production, that leaders of the Japanese auto industry took bold
steps.

In the first half of the 1980s, the business strategy of auto companies was that local production would complement reduced
exports from Japan. After a G-5 meeting of finance ministers in
September 1985 approved an increase in the value of the yen, the
profitability of exports from Japan deteriorated and Japanese car
makers were forced to revise their business strategy so as to put
more emphasis on local production.

With production technology and state-of-the art facilities, North
American plants have become the most important elements in the
global business strategies of Japanese car makers under unfavorable yen-dollar exchanges rates for exporters. In 1999, Japanese
car makers assembled more than three million cars in North
American—2.48 million cars in the United States and 580,000 in
Canada.

3. THE INFUSION OF JAPANESE PRODUCTION SYSTEMS AND
THEIR IMPACT

Japanese companies that were engaged in production in the United
States faced a crucial issue as to how they should transfer the
Japanese way of management, particularly Japanese-style produc-
tion systems, to their North American plants.

As was the case in the Matsushita Quasar plant, the differences
between Japanese and American production systems were enormous. The American mass-production system was based on
assembly lines with each worker responsible for only a single task.
The Japanese system of lean production attached greater importance to teamwork by employees responsible for multiple tasks.

In the American system, quality control was the responsibility of
specialists, and products that failed to meet the quality standards
were excluded at the final section of an assembly line. In the
Japanese system, in contrast, quality control was carried out before

and during production. Production areas as a whole were responsible for quality. Assembly-line workers were encouraged to hold QC meetings and to discuss how to improve quality and production processes.

The two nations' systems also differed in regard to components procurement. In America, manufacturers seeking lower-cost components concluded short-term contracts with suppliers after public bidding. Manufacturers themselves conducted strict quality checks of the components supplied. U.S. manufacturers and suppliers cooperated less with each other than their Japanese counterparts did.

In contrast, the Japanese system was based on long-term partnerships between manufacturers and suppliers. Suppliers tried to reduce costs by streamlining their operations. They gave warranties on their products and strictly observed the designated delivery dates. Under a total-design policy, suppliers themselves designed and tested components. The Japanese way of procuring components was better in terms of efficiency and technology and in maintaining quality.

The biggest challenge for Japanese car manufacturers was how to transfer their production systems to U.S. plants in harmony with the local culture and local labor practices. Any Japanese principles that seemed universal were adopted, and the rest were creatively modified to meet local needs and situations.

Job classification was simplified as much as possible, increasing the responsibilities of workers. At Big Three plants, there were hundreds of different kinds of tasks. At Japanese plants, jobs were integrated into three major categories and workers were encouraged to develop the capacity to handle multiple responsibilities. Teamwork also was emphasized.

Unlike American companies that laid off employees easily, the U.S. plants of Japanese auto companies adopted a no-layoffs policy. However, the Japanese lifetime employment system, which typically was linked with seniority-based wages, was excluded, and the American-style work-hour-based payment system was retained.

In other words, practices that were related to the lifestyles and personal value systems of local employees were respected, and management adapted to them. Japanese-style personnel and work-shift systems were not employed, because they were based on Japanese lifestyles and value systems under which corporations were regarded as part of workers' lives.

Similarly, Japanese-style work-and capacity-evaluation and promotion systems based on workshops were not employed. Instead, team leaders or group leaders were appointed from among employees who wanted to take on such responsibilities and to be promoted. Promotions were made on the basis of evaluations by management.

As to work shifts, unlike the Japanese system, workers were not rotated, and they worked on a fixed shift, either a first or second shift. Based upon seniority, workers were given the right to choose the shift on which to work.

Quality-control circles were not immediately introduced in American plants. Minor activities for improving work environments, including campaigns for keeping work floors clean, tidy, and in order, were first introduced during on-the-job training that aimed at developing workers capacity to perform multiple tasks. As employees' awareness of quality increased, quality-control circles were organized. They have now seemingly taken root in American plants of Japanese car manufacturers, and at world-wide conventions of quality-control circles of Honda and Toyota, workers representing their North American plants report on what they are doing.

Above all, Toyota's experiences in transferring the Japanese-style production system to an American plant operated jointly with GM are noteworthy. It was a closed GM plant in Fremont, California, that Toyota had to deal with. At NUMMI, the Toyota-GM joint venture, the majority of workers were members of the United Automobile Workers (UAW) Union. They had worked under an American-style mass-production system. Efforts were made to fully restructure NUMMI, modeling it after Toyota's Takaoka plant in Japan. Production equipment was replaced and the layout of workshops was changed. Some American employees were sent to Japan for training and became team leaders or group leaders for Toyota-style production.

Soon, representatives of the UAW at NUMMI declared that the union would cooperate with the Japanese management, entering into a labor-management agreement. The union agreed to simplify complicated job classifications into three major categories and to accept training for jobs with multiple responsibilities. It also accepted the just-in-time production system.

To observe how Toyota managed the plant, the GM head office in Detroit sent its top production and procurement executives to NUMMI. They later returned to their offices in Detroit, bringing Toyota's production management know-how to GM's operations. Among GM executives, "NUMMIzation" became a buzzword. Actually, the system for manufacturing the subcompact Saturn cars and those at GM Opel's plants in Germany and Argentina were based on Toyota's production philosophy.

At North American plants of other Japanese automobile companies, Japanese-style production systems and labor practices were also adopted step by step.

Above all, the attempt to transfer Japanese-style supplier systems into the U.S. automotive industry was probably the hardest task that the Japanese car manufacturers faced in the United States. It required efforts to build up partnerships with local suppliers. The target was to establish both a components warranty system by suppliers and a system to give technological and management support to suppliers.

Local suppliers were asked to deliver components following the just-in-time system, and to jointly work with manufacturers to reduce costs on mid- and long-term bases. The suppliers that had technological abilities were asked to jointly work with manufacturers in designing components. The introduction of the Japanese-style systems involving suppliers was accelerated as local plants under Japanese management increased the procurement of local contents. At the initial stage of production, local contents accounted for about 50 percent of the total, and most key components, such as engines, transmissions, and brakes, were purchased from Japan.

Initially, local American suppliers were reluctant to accommodate Japanese car manufacturers' requests for providing product warranties and delivering products several times a day, mainly because order quantities were small. For their part, manufacturers preferred to buy components from suppliers in Japan, because those suppliers were familiar with the Japanese-style production systems and were small-car components specialists.

In their efforts to localize operations, Japanese car manufacturers gradually increased purchasing from local suppliers in the United States. As local components increased, the car manufacturers carried out strict inspections when the supplies arrived. Step by step, they moved toward establishing product-warranty systems, winning the understanding of local suppliers who, by and large, had not allowed quality specialists of Japanese car manufacturers into their factories and had not welcomed their advice. When Japanese manufacturers found problems in supplied components, for example, they successfully persuaded local suppliers to accept inspection of their factories so as to discover the cause of the problems. With such efforts, real partnerships were formed between manufacturers and suppliers, and product-warranty systems were established.

Coincidently, the Big Three, learning from Japanese manufacturers' relations with suppliers, were integrating their suppliers as part of reform programs of their components supply systems. A change in the consciousness of local suppliers followed, making it easier for Japanese car manufacturers to step up the transfer of their supplier systems to their North American plants.

Local contents now account for 75–80 percent of the total components used at the plants of Japanese automobile companies, which is equal to or more than the Big Three's local-contents procurement. *Genchika,* or localization, which started with components procurement, has been progressing, and product development is also now done locally in the Unite States.

Major Japanese automotive companies, including Toyota, Honda, and Nissan, operate local design and development centers that design cars to meet the tastes of North American consumers, exchanging information with their counterparts in Japan. Honda's Accord was one such model that was developed by the collaboration of Japanese and American designers and engineers. Every part of the car's development process—designing of production platforms, body style, and the interior and exterior of the car—was handled by local teams.

4. THE REVIVAL OF U.S. COMPANIES AND THE EFFECT OF JAPANESE-STYLE MANAGEMENT ON THEM

The experiences of automobile and auto-parts companies were discussed in the previous section. They are the most distinguished cases among Japanese companies that ventured to produce in the United States.

Throughout the 1980s, Japanese automobile companies built manufacturing plants in North America one after another, infusing the Japanese way of management, particularly Japanese production systems, into their local operations. In the first half of the 1980s, their North American plants contributed to maintaining Japanese car sales in the United States while car exports from Japan were voluntarily regulated. In the second half of the 1980s, they became the mainstay of the Japanese car trade in the North American market, because exporting from Japan became less profitable due to the rapid appreciation of the yen vis-à-vis the U.S. dollar.

Local components, which had accounted for only 50 percent of all parts, increased to 75 percent or more. The North American plants of Japanese car manufacturers produced more than three million cars a year. Japanese car makers and components manufacturers created more than 200,000 jobs in North America.

In the 1990s, when globalization took place in the world's auto industry, the North American plants became an indispensable part of global business for the Japanese automobile makers.

How did the Big Three American car companies respond to the Japanese move? What did they learn, if anything, from the Japanese? Did they creatively utilize what they learned, in order to revive themselves?

Although each of the Big Three reacted differently, what was common among them was that they made efforts to adopt Japanese methods as much as possible. Among Japanese systems that the Big Three introduced were quality-control circles and *kaizen* or improvement techniques, minimization of components inventories, making metal-pressing work more flexible by integrating it into assembling processes at plants, changes of assembling arrangements, easier-to-work-on shop-floor layouts, and the change of supplier systems. They also reformed their product-development systems and relations with suppliers, referring to the Japanese systems.

Chrysler, for instance, adopted a concurrent engineering system and successfully shortened the product-development time. Using IT technology, a global network of suppliers was successfully created, combining the benefits of the network system and the Japanese *keiretsu* system.

Of course, some Japanese-style systems were not introduced because of opposition from labor unions. These included the simplification of job classifications and the training of workers to perform jobs involving multiple tasks, which would lead to the loss of jobs for some workers.

The net result was that the Big Three, quickly adopting some of Japanese systems while also creating their own systems, returned to profitability in the 1990s. Ford and Chrysler concentrated their management resources on the markets for mini-vans, pick-up trucks, and sports utility vehicles, which Japanese car manufacturers under-evaluated, while the Japanese companies remained focused on the sedans market. The U.S. automobile companies, whose marketing strategies were successful, came back as corporations with higher profitability. The long-lasting boom of the U.S. economy and the expansion of the global economy helped their comeback. Thus, the high strategy-making abilities of the Big Three, utilizing IT technology, resulted in such visible achievements.

In contrast, the competitiveness of the Japanese automobile makers declined in the 1990s, due to a long recession in Japan after the burst of the economic bubble in the early 1990s and the economic crisis of Asia in 1997. Particularly those Japanese auto companies that failed to develop good strategies lost ground in the auto market and in the overall global reformation of the automotive industry.

However, the North American assembly plants of Japanese car companies now are deeply rooted in their local markets and will continue to be important elements of the global strategies of Japanese automotive companies. What Japanese auto companies and components manufacturers now require is the ability to develop sound strategies that can meet the changes in globalization, plus the ability to move systematically and quickly using IT technology. This is what the Japanese companies should learn from the experiences of American auto companies.

Chapter 4

JAPANESE AMERICANS SINCE WORLD WAR II

MASAKO IINO

INTRODUCTION

The history of Japanese Americans shows that the status of
Japanese Americans in American society has been greatly influenced
by the ups and downs of relations between the United States and
Japan. Such influence of U.S.–Japan relations on the status of
Japanese Americans in American society is most clearly observed
when those relations deteriorate. The best example of this is the
American government's decision during World War II to remove
Japanese Americans from the West Coast and to intern them in
relocation centers. This policy made all Japanese Americans aware
of the close relationship between the United States and Japan and
in the most extreme situation, as well as of the relationship between
themselves and Japan.

For Japanese Americans, the postwar period, which started
under such conditions, was a period of important changes that also
has been closely related to the changing relations between the
United States and Japan. Even in the 1960s, two decades after the
war's end, many *Issei* would not tell their children their own experiences of having been interned, and many *Nisei* were not willing to
learn the Japanese language so as to better communicate with their

parents. These cases reflect the influence of deteriorated relations between the United States and Japan. Many Japanese Americans were ashamed of their Japanese origin and had a sense of guilt, or they felt that they were stigmatized because of their experiences during the war.

However, although it might seem to contradict the above example, after the war many Japanese Americans were concerned about the conditions in Japan, which had been defeated. Such Japanese Americans contributed to the LARA (Licensed Agencies for Relief in Asia) Program, which sent relief supplies to war-stricken Japan from 1946 through 1952. It is quite impressive that Japanese Americans, who had been interned and were still struggling to reestablish themselves in unfamiliar environments, were engaged in helping people in Japan, and were thus confirming their ties with Japan immediately after the war, in which their identity had been questioned in such a cruel manner.

In recent years, the third and the fourth generations of Japanese Americans (*Sansei* and *Yonsei*, respectively) have demonstrated their concerns regarding U.S.–Japan relations. This tendency reflects both the recent conditions of U.S.–Japan relations and such changes in American society as the rise of multiculturalism. One conspicuous example of such cases is that Japanese Americans themselves felt the impact of the so-called Japan bashing in the 1980s and early 1990s. They felt that Japan bashing turned into "Japanese American bashing." The important factor in this situation is that Japanese Americans came to actively involve themselves in efforts to improve the relations between the two countries, with a sense of mission that they are the ones who could be a bridge between the United States and Japan.

In this essay I investigate the situation of Japanese Americans after World War II, examining the cases mentioned above.

1. JAPANESE AMERICANS IMMEDIATELY AFTER THE WAR

In the postwar period, some interesting events that reflected the deteriorating relations between the United States and Japan occurred. The Japanese American Citizens League (JACL), an organization that was in the position of leading the Japanese American community at that time, tried to convince Japanese Americans to cooperate with the evacuation procedures of the American government. The JACL's official creed, which was read into the Congressional Record in 1941, clearly shows the stand that the JACL took at the time of war with Japan. In part it says the following:

> Because I believe in America, and I trust she believes in me, and because I have received innumerable benefits from her, I pledge myself to do honor to her at all times and in all places; to support her Constitution, to obey her laws, to respect her flag; to defend her against all enemies, foreign or domestic; to assume actively my duties and obligations as a citizen, cheerfully and without any reservation whatsoever, in the hope that I may become a better American in a greater America.[1]

It was only natural that the JACL leaders were often condemned by many Japanese Americans, particularly the *Issei* and the *Kibei* (second-generation Japanese Americans who were educated in Japan during their formative years), for "selling the Japanese communities down the river." The *Issei* and the *Kibei* suffered from an identity dilemma, because they were Japanese subjects—subjects of an enemy country—living in the United States.

Many scholars have argued that the internment also affected the *Nisei*—who were citizens of the United States—in regard to their self-image and ethnic identity. Many of them, it has been argued, came to be ashamed of being of Japanese origin and tried to separate themselves from things Japanese, or tried to hide the fact that they were related to Japan. Or they tried to remove themselves from things that might make them or the people around them recognize that they were of Japanese origin. Some even decided not speak to their parents in Japanese, even though they realized that Japanese was the only language by which they could really communicate with their parents.

In other words, because of their experiences during the war, many *Nisei* came to have not only a sense of disillusionment toward the government of their own country, but also a sense of guilt; in other words, they carried a stigma with them. Some *Nisei* have described their experience as "being punished," because they felt they had done "something wrong."

Some Japanese Americans, however, were more concerned with the situation of the Japanese in Japan than with their own condition in their own country.

2. THE LARA RELIEF ACTIVITIES

When World War II ended with Japan's surrender, Japan was completely destroyed and devastated, as a defeated country always is. The majority of Japanese experienced difficulty in securing food and clothing sufficient to allow them to survive. It was to Japan in this situation that relief supplies were sent by LARA.

According to the Japanese government's report titled "LARA *Kyūen Busshi ni tsuite*" (Concerning LARA Relief Supplies),[2] as of November 1950, the Japanese government had received through LARA 13,190 tons of food, clothing, medical supplies, shoes, soap, raw materials, and other items, as well as 2,175 goats and 45 milk cows. If these supplies could be converted into yen, their value was more than ¥ four billion.

In Japan those relief supplies were received and processed by the Japanese government under the supervision of the Allied General Headquarters (GHQ) until the LARA Central Committee was established by the Ministry of Welfare (the present Ministry of Health, Labor and Welfare) in March 1950. The committee was composed of 22 members, including 3 representatives of LARA and some members from the Ministry of Welfare. The committee was expected to fulfill the purpose of distributing the supplies "equally, effectively, promptly and appropriately," to those who needed them. The number of those who benefited from the LARA relief supplies reached 17,000,000 by the end of 1950.

Thirteen organizations—some of them were religious, and others were social work or labor organizations—made up LARA:

American Federation of Labor
American Friends Service Committee
Brethren Service Committee

Catholic War Relief Service
Christian Rural Overseas Project
Christian Science Service Committee
Church World Service
Congress of Industrial Organizations
Lutheran World Relief
Mennonite Central Committee Akron, Pennsylvania
Salvation Army
Unitarian Service Committee
People with good will and altruistic intentions in the United States, Canada, and South America contacted one of these organizations and contributed relief supplies to it, and LARA collected and sent them to devastated Japan.

What should be noted here is that about 20 percent of all the relief supplies were contributed by Japanese Americans and Japanese Canadians, as well as by people of Japanese origin in South America. As early as immediately after the end of the war, many Americans were concerned with the situation in Europe and started to send relief supplies to Europe. Those good-willed Americans were exclusively interested in sending relief supplies to European countries. It was people of Japanese origin who directed Americans' attention to the situation in Japan and started and promoted a system that enabled the supplies to be sent to Japan.

According to *"Beishū Kakkoku no Zairyū Dōhō ni yotte Kessei Sareta Kyūsai-dantai Shirabe"* (Survey of Relief Organizations Organized by Overseas Countrymen in the Americas),[3] a survey conducted by the Japanese Ministry of Foreign Affairs in response to a request of the Ministry of Welfare in 1952, there were 36 organizations of people of Japanese origin in North and South America that contributed to this relief program. Some of them were originally social and friendship organizations and later started relief activities, and others were newly born after the war with the specific purpose of sending relief supplies to Japan. They included such organizations as the following:
Beikoku Seihoku-bu Nihon Nanmin Kyūsai-kai (Northwest Area Association for the Relief of Displaced People in Japan) (Seattle)

Brazil Sekijūji-Kōnin Nihon Sensai Dōhō Kyūen-kai (Brazil Association Officially Recognized by the Red Cross for the Relief of War Victims in Japan) (Rio de Janeiro)

Chicago Nikkei Dantai Rengo Shusai Nihon Nanmin Iinkai (Chicago Committee for the Relief of Displaced People in Japan Sponsored by Associations of Japanese Americans) (Chicago)

Cleveland Kokoku Nanmin Kyūsai-kai (Cleveland Association for Relief of Displaced People in Our Homeland) (Cleveland)

Hakkō-kai (Honolulu)

Hawaii Dōshi-kai (Hawaii Comrades Association) (Honolulu)

LARA Nihon Nanmin Kyūsai Iinkai (LARA Committee for Relief of Displaced People in Japan) (Honolulu)

Maui Nihon Nanmin Kyūsai Iinkai (Maui Committee for the Relief of Displaced People in Japan) (Wailuku)

Nihon Nanmin Kyūsai-kai (Association for the Relief of Displaced People in Japan) (Washington, D.C.)

Nihon Nanmin Kyūsai-kai (Association for the Relief of Displaced People in Japan) (San Francisco)

Nihon Kyūsai Nyū-yōku Iinkai (New York Japanese American Committee for Japanese Relief, Inc, which later became the Japanese American Association in New York)

Nikkei Shimin Kyōkai (Japanese American Citizens Association) (Toronto)

Okinawa Kyūsai-kai (Okinawa Relief Association) (Rio de Janeiro)

Ontario Nihon Kyūsai Iinkai (Ontario Committee for Japanese Relief) (Toronto)

Sensai Koji Kyūsai Club (Relief Club for War-Victimized Children) (Honolulu)

Yūai Jūji-kai Hawaii Shibu (Friends Cross Association, Hawaii Branch) (Honolulu)

How, then, did Japanese Americans involve themselves in the relief activities? According to the 1948–49 version of the *New York Bulletin*,[4] published by the Japanese Association of New York, 9 Japanese and Japanese Americans who were living in New York City "sent out a circular to Japanese Americans in the city, inviting them" to a meeting called *Yūshī Kondankai* (a get-together of those who are interested). This was the beginning of the relief activities of Japanese Americans—on September 5, 1945, only three days after Japan's prime minister signed the instrument of surrender on the battleship Missouri.

On September 14, the *New York Bulletin* records, "[A]bout 40 Japanese Americans, both *Issei* and *Nisei*, responding to this circular, gathered at a Methodist Church, in the heavy rain." They discussed the "possibility of forming an organization whose purpose would be to give relief goods to Japan." Their desire to help Japanese in Japan, however, did not materialize at that time, which was a time when *Issei* were still looked upon as "enemy aliens" and "were not allowed to even to get together, even though the war was over." Banks would not accept any contributions that were not approved by the government's relief-control committee in Washington, D.C. It was "prohibited to send any goods or money to Japan." They could not start any sort of relief activity at that time.

Those who were at the meeting could do nothing more than to set up a preparatory committee to "proceed with the study of the situation and to choose committee members." According to the record of the meeting, the committee was composed of 20 members, including some *Nisei*. This shows that although many *Nisei* rejected their ties with Japan, considering it a "stigma," there were exceptions. There were some *Nisei* who thought that they should do something for the country of their parents.

Immediately after the meeting, however, the possibility of a change in the government's policy was reported. In May, 1946, the preparatory committee then held another meeting, at a church in New York City. At that meeting was proposed the establishment of a solid organization whose major purpose would be to give relief goods to Japanese in Japan. The proposal was accepted by those present at the meeting, and it was decided that an office was to be set up. In August 1946, the New York Japanese American Committee for Japan Relief was approved as a corporation under New York state law. At the same time, it became possible to send relief supplies to Japan through LARA. Then, in September, the new organization formally started its activities and launched a fund-raising campaign. The record shows that the organization succeeded in raising more than $48,000 by the end of that year.

Toward the end of that year, the committee, with the cooperation of the American Friends Service Committee in Philadelphia, started collecting contributions of clothing and other materials. In addition the New York Entertainment Program to Help the Homeland was formed, and in March 1947 it put on a show in that city, collecting a net profit of more than $5,200. In the following year, a similar show was held. It made a net profit of $2,600 to contribute. By then, because sending relief packages to Japan by methods other than through LARA was legally allowed, the amount of contributions which the organization collected was not as much as in the first year of the campaign. Still, by September 1947, the total amount of relief supplies sent to Japan by the American Friends Service Committee totaled $561,000 of the total contributions, which in the form of money amounted to $312,000, 70 percent of which were given by Japanese Americans.

In California, where Japanese Americans who had left relocation centers were beginning to return, there also was a call to send relief supplies to Japan. On October 24, 1945, shortly after the aforementioned meeting in New York, some Japanese Americans formed an organization called Nanka Nihon Nanmin Kyūsai-kai (Southern California Relief Organization for Displaced People in Japan) in Los Angeles. In San Francisco, Kokoku Kyūsai Sōdan-kai (Conference to Discuss Relief for the Homeland) was held in November, and Nihon Nanmin Kyūsai-kai (Association for the Relief of Displaced People in Japan) was formed in January of the following year. *Kikan Fukkō Shi* (History of Returned People and Their Reestablishment), published by Nichibei Times Publishing Co. in San Francisco, tells how Japanese Americans, who had just returned from relocation centers and were still struggling to establish themselves, stood up to help Japanese in Japan:

> Those Japanese Americans who returned could find literally no houses to live in. Some of them were lucky enough to rent a room in Whites' houses. Others had to sleep in single beds arranged in rows in the basements or halls of so-called hostels,

newly prepared in churches and meeting halls. They were exactly like displaced people. To them in such a situation, news describing the situation in Japan was brought little by little by military people staying in Japan in the Occupation Army or by newspaper correspondents. They all depicted the desperate situation of poverty-stricken people in Japan immediately after Japan surrendered.

Fellow countrymen [Japanese Americans], who learned of the situation in Japan through this news, typically described their feelings as follows:

> "Although we experienced isolated lives in the concentration camps, deprived of our freedom, we never experienced the lack of food and clothing. However, we heard that, in contrast, war victims in our homeland, Japan, had lost their houses and were unable to obtain even bread. We, their blood relatives, could not bear to see their difficulties. We gathered together and looked for ways to save them from such a situation.

> "Then we started to discuss what we could do. Our desire to give a helping hand gradually grew."[5]

The purpose of the organization Nihon Nanmin Kyūsai-kai in San Francisco was expressed in its prospectus, which was written by Mr. Shichinosuke Asano, publisher of the Japanese language newspaper *Nichibei Times*. Mr. Asano eventually came to work as the secretary of the organization. Those who started the organization learned that "the war victims in Japan did not have food to survive on, or clothing to keep themselves warm, nor even places to shelter themselves from wind and rain, and there was no knowing how many were on the verge of starvation when the severe winter approached." They "could not help taking pity on them." They "felt an urge to do something—they could not stay without taking any action"—and accordingly they formed an organization.

It was their "conscientious sense of duty" to help Japanese in such a situation that moved them, as "they, reflecting upon their own situation, considered themselves rather fortunate as they had enough to eat and had something to spare for others." They felt they should help Japanese in Japan "even if they had to share a meal with others and to give up some part of a small stipend." It is interesting to note that this activity was, for those Japanese Americans, a way of reciprocating for the contributions they had received from Japanese in Japan during their internment. The prospectus says that "they recollect how they, in relocation centers, were moved and touched by such comfort articles as medicine, books, and toys, as well as *shōyu* and *miso*, sent by their countrymen," and that "they recollect the warm kindness Japanese people who were in destitute showed" to Japanese Americans "whose food, clothing, and housing were secured." With such memories, "they could not help but to willingly share what they had with those living in poverty in Japan."[6]

The Pacific War brought Japanese Americans unmeasurable hardships. For them, the starting point of the 50 years after the end of World War II was to give helping hands to poverty-stricken people in their homeland across the Pacific, through LARA. At the same time, it is true that until the 1970s, when the redress movement was launched, some *Nisei* felt they had a negative self-image as being of Japanese origin, and they remained silent about their experiences. However, there were Japanese Americans who regarded their ties to Japan as very important, even when they themselves were going through very difficult times.

3. THE SUCCESS OF THE REDRESS MOVEMENT

The Japanese Americans who experienced the Civil Rights Movement in the 1960s gradually came to discard their stigmatized view of themselves as being of Japanese origin and started to see their ties to Japan in a positive light. The important background to this concerned changes in American society. For example, the Civil Rights Movement greatly influenced the attitude of the American public toward the problems of minorities. Another important element was that the social and economic status of Japanese Americans rose to a level such that they were labeled a "model minority." The fact that Japan was making great economic progress at the time, resulting in good U.S.–Japan relations, also contributed to the change in the self-image of Japanese Americans and their ties to Japan.

Monetary compensation for property losses caused by the evacuation was, in an incomplete way, effected by the passage of the Evacuation Claims Act of 1948, which was signed into law by President Truman. Pursuant to this act, after years of complex procedures, a total of $36,874,240 was paid by the federal government to 26,558 Japanese Americans as compensation for their $400,000,000 in property losses in 1942. The payments were completed in 1965. The Evacuation Claims Act, however, had many serious shortcomings—the amount of payments, the claim-filing procedure, and limited definition of property for which compensation was allowed. Also, the evacuees were never compensated for many properties such as business supplies on furniture, for the money they would have earned had they not been interned, or for the psychological damage they suffered as a result of internment.

After the Evacuation Claims Act, no other action was taken to redress the internment. However, the ethnic and civil rights movements that gained momentum in the late 1960s raised the political consciousness of Japanese Americans. At the 1970 national JACL convention in Chicago, a resolution calling for redress as an issue of the JACL was introduced, although there was not much enthusiasm or support in the JACL to look into the matter of reparations. But, at the JACL national convention in 1974, the National Redress Committee was organized. Its mission was to petition the American government to admit its mistake of imprisonment, detention, and denial of civil and constitutional rights of Japanese Americans during the war. There was, however, still strong opposition to the redress idea, even among many national JACL leaders. Redress was still a controversial subject, and no definite consensus was reached on whether to pursue the issue.

A significant breakthrough came in late 1978, when the nation's first Day of Remembrance, whose purpose was to recognize the Japanese Americans' internment-camp experiences, was held in Seattle. This event left a strong impression not only on the more than 2,000 participants, but on Japanese American communities across the nation. In the following year, similar Day of Remembrance events took place in Portland, San Francisco, and Los Angeles. These events were significant in obtaining the official support of local governments, such as city of Seattle, as well as in receiving wide coverage in the media. Support from the Japanese American population increased and began to have an important influence on the American government.

In 1980, President Carter signed a bill that created the Commission on Wartime Relocation and Internment of Civilians, which in 1981 started 20-day hearings in Washington, D.C., Los Angeles, San Francisco, Seattle, Chicago, New York, and other cities. More than 750 people, including Japanese Americans who had been interned, former government officials, and scholars who had researched the subject, testified before the commission. These hearings received media coverage as well as the attention of Japanese Americans themselves. Japanese Americans stepped forward to make their experiences public and to seek redress from the American government. The redress movement started to progress in 1983, after the commission's report, "Personal Justice Denied,"[7] was issued. The report concluded that internment was based on "race prejudice, war hysteria, and a failure of political leadership."

On August 10, 1988, President Reagan signed the Civil Liberties Act of 1988, a redress bill that provided an official apology and payment of $20,000 to each surviving Japanese American who had been interned during World War II. It also established a public-education fund to inform the public about the internment. The primary purpose of the act was to "acknowledge the fundamental injustice of the evacuation, relocation, and internment of United State citizens and permanent resident aliens of Japanese ancestry during World War II."

The progress of the redress movement in the 1970s and its successful conclusion in 1988 had a major impact on the self-image of Japanese Americans. For Japanese Americans, a more important result of the settlement of the redress issue than the monetary compensation was that it officially erased the stigma that had been attached to them for so many years. The settlement made clear that being of Japanese origin need not give rise to a sense of shame or guilt. Japanese Americans could now relate their wartime experiences to their children and grandchildren with pride. By 1995, 82,598 Japanese Americans had received monetary compensation.[8]

4. "JAPAN BASHING" AND JAPANESE AMERICANS

In the 1980s, the term "Japan bashing" was frequently employed in describing the attitudes of the American public toward Japan and Japanese people, as well as toward Japanese products. Some argued that Japan bashing was a phenomenon that was limited to Washington, D.C. However, in areas with large Japanese American populations, such as California, an increase in so-called hate crimes made Japanese Americans sensitive to their minority status and the possible need to defend themselves against acts of discrimination or even violence. For them the impact of Japan bashing was a reality. Already in 1982 it was reported that anti-Japan and anti-Japanese feelings caused by U.S.–Japan trade friction "were again having a serious influence on Japanese Americans." Mike Masaoka, one of the founders and one-time president of the JACL, in describing the conspicuous similarities between the 1930s and the early 1980s, declared that the "U.S.–Japan relationship is the worst that it has been since World War II, except that Japan is not a military threat to the United States now."

The Vincent Chin incident, in which a young, second-generation Chinese American was beaten to death by two laid-off employees of an auto company in Detroit in 1982, clearly shows that anti-Japan and anti-Japanese feelings could be turned against Japanese Americans. In Detroit, where the unemployment rate was high at the time, auto workers were resentful of Japan and Japanese, who were associated with Japanese-car imports. In that incident, when the two laid-off autoworkers were beating Vincent Chin with a baseball bat, they were overheard calling him "Jap." The Chinese American in this incident was taken for a Japanese American. A member of the JACL is reported to have said on the occasion of the Vincent Chin incident that "it is always Japanese Americans who are made scapegoats when the relations between the United States and Japan deteriorate," because the general American public makes no distinction between Japanese and Japanese Americans. Many Japanese Americans say that they "continue to suffer from the misconceptions that led to the internment of their parents or grandparents."[11] The *Los Angeles Times* reported that even in the 1990s the Japanese American community was "feeling the effects of furor over the trade imbalance."[12] In this way the Japanese American community has felt the strong impact and implications of Japan bashing.

5. "A BRIDGE BETWEEN THE UNITED STATES AND JAPAN"

According to the 1990 U.S. Census, foreign-born Japanese Americans constitute 32.4% of the total Japanese American population, which is a much smaller percentage than for other Asian groups (over 60%). Unlike most other Asian groups, the Japanese have not been immigrating to the United States in significant numbers in recent years. Although not much research has been conducted on the so-called *Shin-Issei*, postwar Japanese immigrants, it has been a shared view that both the *Sansei* and *Yonsei* who belong to the same age cohort of *Shin-Issei*, and the *Issei* and *Nisei* who look back on Japan with nostalgia, keep apart from *Shin-Issei*. Difference in their backgrounds seem to have kept them from associating with each other.

In the 1990s, however, the distance between the two groups has become less than it was in the 1980s. For example, Nobiru-kai, an organization of *Shin-Issei* in San Francisco, has been involved in the activities of both older Japanese Americans and Japanese businesspeople in the area. In this case, cooperation has been observed among Japanese Americans who have been in the United States for a long period of time, *Shin-Issei* who settled there recently, and Japanese businesspeople. This clearly shows that many Japanese Americans are willing to look at their ties to Japan.

Their attitude reveals their belief that they should help to improve U.S.–Japan relations by serving as a bridge between the United States and Japan. The idea of a bridge between the United States and Japan was not new in the 1990s. In 1925 and 1926, groups of *Nisei* were sent to Japan by Nisei Kengakudan, which was organized by Kyūtaro Abiko, a respected *Issei* leader who founded the Japanese newspaper *Nichibei* in California, was based on the same idea. Abiko claimed that communication and education should be the ways to be taken in order to solve the problem of Japanese immigrants in the United States, and that *Nisei* should play an important role as a bridge between the United States and Japan. According to him, the first step toward realizing his idea was that *Nisei* should visit Japan and learn more about that country.

The idea in the 1990s of *Nisei* becoming a bridge between the United States and Japan was not exactly the same as that of Abiko. The important difference is that the idea is now advocated by the *Sansei* themselves. They believe that they should be the ones who play such a role. Their awareness of their being in a position where they can understand the situations both in the United States and in Japan, and being capable of becoming a bridge has been displayed in their recent acts. This is a change of great importance observed recently in the Japanese American community. Japanese Americans who have been passively swayed by changes in the U.S.–Japan relations and yet who have not stood up for either country, are now expressing their wish to play that important role and are expressing their confidence in being able to do so.

Many of the events and activities in Japanese American communities in the 1990s revealed that Japanese Americans were conscious of their history since the end of World War II. For example, in 1995, one of the World War II internment camps was reproduced and exhibited in Little Tokyo in Los Angeles. A number of tours to visit the sites of former internment camps were scheduled, and symposiums regarding the wartime experiences of Japanese Americans as their themes were organized in the 1990s. This shows that Japanese Americans consider the years since the end of World War II important to them, and, at the same time, that with the redress settlement they started to present their history and their identity to the public in a positive way.

In 1995, it was reported in the media that a piece of land in Washington, D.C. was officially approved as a site for a monument commemorating Japanese Americans' patriotism during World War II. In 1999, a ground-breaking ceremony was held at this site, and the media reported that 10 Japanese Americans, each of whom had lived in 1 of the 10 relocation camps during the war, were invited to shovel soil at the ceremony, and that cherry trees were to be planted there as a symbol of peace and ties to Japan.

In 1997, the Japanese American National Museum started a new three-year project, called the International Nikkei Research Project. It aims to explore, beyond national boundaries, the rich and diverse culture of people of Japanese ancestry across the world. More than 20 researchers from North and South America, Hawaii, and Japan have participated in the project in order to record the experiences of people of Japanese ancestry internationally and globally, and to offer that record to the world. The existence of such a project itself reflects the fact that Japanese Americans regard their ties to Japan positively.

In October 2000, a newly born nonprofit organization called the Japanese American Community Leadership Council in California sent, with the support of the Japanese Ministry of Foreign Affairs, 12 *Sansei* to Japan. The aim of their visit was, according to the statement issued by the council, "to improve relations between Japanese Americans and Japan, to find ways to promote the roles that Japanese Americans, particularly *Sansei* and *Yonsei*, can play in creating a closer relationship between the United States and Japan, and to establish a foundation for exchanges between Japanese Americans and Japanese." Japanese Americans who have been swayed by the waves of U.S.–Japan relations now see Japan and their ties to Japan with a new consciousness and a new awareness.

NOTES:

1. Bill Hosokawa, *JACL in Quest of Justice: the History of the Japanese American Citizens League* (New York: William Morrow and Co., Inc., 1982), pp. 279–80.

2. Bureau of Social Policy, Ministry of Welfare, *LARA Kyūen Busshi ni tsuite* [Concerning LARA Relief Supplies] (January, 1951), p. 7.

3. Ministry of Foreign Affairs, "Beishū Kakkoku no Zairyū Dōhō ni yotte Kessei sareta Kyūsai-dantai Shirabe [A Survey of Relief Organizations Organized by Overseas Countrymen in the Americas], *Documents*.

4. New York Japanese Society, *Nyū Yōku Binran* [New York Bulletin], 1948–49, p. 53.

5. *Kaigai Nikkei-jin* [Nikkei People Overseas], 36 (May 1995), pp. 10–11.

6. Ministry of Foreign Affairs, "Sengo Nanboku-Bei no Zairyū-dōhō ni yotte Kessei sareta Kyūsai-dantai no Chōsa ni kansuru Ken [On a Survey of Relief Organizations Organized by Overseas Countrymen in North and South America after WW II], *Documents*.

7. Commission on Wartime Relocation and Internment of Civilians, *Report: Personal Justice Denied* (Washington, D.C., 1982), p. 10.

8. *Pacific Citizen*, February 3–16, 1995.

9. *Asahi Shimbun* [Newspaper], June 4, 1982.

10. Ibid.

11. *Los Angeles Times*, February 21, 1992.

12. Ibid.

Chapter 5

THE ROLE OF THE AMERICA–JAPAN SOCIETY, INC.

AKIKO KUNO

"On behalf of our delegation leaving shortly for San Francisco to attend the International Conference for the signing of a Japanese peace treaty, I desire to express our heartfelt gratitude to the America–Japan Society for arranging this magnificent send-off." said then-Prime Minister Shigeru Yoshida as he began a speech at a luncheon held by the America–Japan Society on August 28, 1951. Among those in the audience were General Matthew B. Ridgeway, who had just succeeded General MacArthur as the Supreme Commander of Allied Forces, and General Ridgeway's political advisor William J. Sebald.

In his speech, Yoshida expressed gratitude to the United States for welcoming the vanquished nation back into the international community as a sovereign state upholding freedom and equality. Going back in history, Yoshida commended America for first having freed Japan from centuries of isolation imposed by the Edo shogunate and for liberating it again—from decades of militarism that had separated the country from the rest of the world. Asserting that these events weren't just coincidences in the history, he said that the two countries are bound by a common destiny.

In conclusion, he said, "Let me conclude by thanking again the America–Japan Society for this delightful luncheon, and wishing it success in its high mission to cultivate Japanese–American friendly relations and thereby to contribute to the cause of world peace and prosperity."

Yoshida was leading a delegation on which had been bestowed the awesome mission of signing treaties that would enable Japan to step out in the world once again as an independent nation. If so, why wasn't the government holding a farewell party? Why did a private organization such as the America–Japan Society get the honor of sponsoring the luncheon? To explain why, we must go back to the beginnings of the society.

The origin of the America–Japan Society goes back a long way, to the period of World War I. U.S.–Japan relations were full of tension relating to China, especially after Japan presented its "21 Demands" in May of 1915. To prevent deterioration of bilateral ties, Japanese scholars who had studied in the United Sates during the Meiji era, and others who were interested in maintaining friendly relations, got together with Americans living in Tokyo with the intent of forming a private organization for promoting friendly relations between the two nations.

Their efforts culminated in creation of the America–Japan Society in April of 1917, the same year in which the two countries signed a joint declaration of friendship known as the Ishii–Lansing Agreement. Kentaro Kaneko, author of the Meiji Constitution and the first Japanese graduate of Harvard, was chosen as the society's first president. The title of honorary president went to then-American ambassador Roland S. Morris. The roster of honorary vice-president was filled with some of the top names of the time in Japanese politics, business, and academia, including Tokugawa Ietatsu, Eiichi Shibusawa, Korekiyo Takahashi and Jōkichi Takamine. The council members included Inazō Nitobe, Kijūrō Shidehara, Takuma Dan, Seihin Ikeda, and Junnosuke Inoue. That impressive list is a testimonial to the fact that U.S.–Japan relations were a matter of great interest and concern for Japanese in leadership positions at the time.

In the years since its formation, the America–Japan Society has become involved in a variety of projects whose aim was the promotion of friendship between the two nations. After the 1923 Great Kanto Earthquake, the society became a destination for substantial amounts of donations sent by Americans. It also acted as a host for the

American fleet, which arrived with doctors, nurses, and emergency supplies.

The society was an indispensable vehicle for bilateral exchanges of all sorts. American dignitaries and celebrities, including Charles Lindbergh and Babe Ruth, who visited Japan before World War II, were almost always invited to address the society.

With the arrival of the Showa era in 1926, however, Japan began leaning toward fascism, as its civilian government faced challenges from the military in attempted coups in 1932 and again in 1936. Despite the efforts by the founders of the society to maintain friendship with Americans, the country would eventually go down the path to the war with China and the United States.

On a notable occasion in October 1939, then-U.S. Ambassador Joseph Grew delivered the famous "straight from the horse's mouth" speech to the society. In it, he said the American government and people were fully aware of what Japan was up to in China, and bluntly warned that the only way to save the bilateral relationship was to face up to those facts and to find solutions.

In 1940, the society's Vice-President Aysuke Kabayama addressed the American people through a radio broadcast, saying that all that Japan wanted in Asia was peace and stability, and that the two countries, by working together for greater economic cooperation, could avoid a war that would be detrimental to both.

With the beginning of the Pacific War, the society was naturally forced to cease all activities. But as soon as the war was over, the society's prewar directors got together and in 1946 opened a temporary office to plan a resumption of its activities under the Allied occupation. The society held its first postwar general meeting in June 1948, to revise its by-laws so as to conform to the democratic era in Japan.

During the postwar decades, which were first marked by economic and social chaos and later by rapid economic growth, there were few other Japanese organizations with the ability to host American visitors and to hold lectures in English. For that reason, the society often became a venue for American officials to enunciate U.S. policy toward Japan.

Then-Vice-President Richard Nixon, for example, chose the America–Japan Society luncheon in November 1953 to lay the groundwork for the close alliance that later became the hallmark of bilateral ties under the Mutual Security Treaty. Nixon talked of a need to confront the threat of communism and to achieve peace, and he argued that Japan must rebuild its military forces to an appropriate level so as to become a fortress for defense of the free world.

The society also played an important role in many educational and cultural exchange programs. Between 1954 and 1969, the society was in charge of selecting candidates to participate in Harvard University's summer international studies seminars, at the behest of then-Professor Henry Kissinger. Many of the fellows in the program later achieved prominent positions in Japanese politics, business, and academia. For those and other Japanese students and researchers aspiring to study in the United States under a Fulbright fellowship, the College Women's Club, and other programs, the society held a farewell party each year at the Mitsui Club in Tokyo.

As a part of its effort to introduce traditional Japanese art to the American public, the Society took the lead in raising money for construction of a classical wooden Japanese house in the courtyard of New York's Museum of Modern Art. With additional financial help from John D. Rockefeller III, the Shofuso, as the house is known, was completed in 1954. The structure was later transported to the Fairmont Park in Philadelphia, where it attracts 10,000 visitors each year.

The society has worked with other organizations to sponsor various events to commemorate milestones in the history of interaction between Japan and the United States since the arrival of Perry's Black Ships. These include the Shimoda Black Ship Festival, the *Kanrin Maru* Festival to commemorate the first official Japanese delegation to the United States, which traveled on a ship bearing that name, and the centennial of the 1858 Trade and Friendship Agreement.

As Japan's role in the international community expanded along with the rise of its economic strength, a number of other private organizations were formed to promote friendship between Japan and the United States. In recent years, local governments and communities have become actively involved in international exchange programs of their own, making new contributions to mutual understanding between the two nations.

To network various efforts by local communities, the National Association of the America–Japan Societies was formed in the 1980s, and it began organizing exchange programs jointly with

Japan–America Societies in the United States. In 1995, Japanese and American members of the societies in both countries first met in a symposium in Hawaii to commemorate the 50th anniversary of the end of World War II. During this epoch-making event, hosted by the Japan–America Society of Hawaii, participants agreed to make it a tradition to hold similar symposia, alternating the venue between the two countries. The second such symposium was held in Fukuoka in May 1998, and the third one, to mark the 50th anniversary of signing of the San Francisco Peace Treaties, is scheduled for September 2001 in San Francisco.

As we stand at the beginning of 21st century, we are confident that the network of Japan–America Societies in both countries will continue to host activities, designed to maintain and build trust between people of the two countries, so that both nations will enjoy peace and prosperity. That is exactly what the founders aimed for when they created the society.

Chapter 6

JAPANESE CULTURE IN THE UNITED STATES:

Japanese Cuisine Making Its Way

YŪZABURŌ MOGI

1. INTRODUCTION

No fewer than 400 Japanese restaurants operate in New York City at present.

In early 1980, they reportedly totaled only about 200. In the last two decades, the number of New York restaurants offering Japanese cuisine has doubled. In the later half of the 1950s, when I was studying in the United States, there were only 7 Japanese restaurants in New York City, and most of the customers were either Japanese Americans or Japanese expatriates. Now, the majority of diners are local Americans.

Menus, too, have undergone quite a few changes as the popularity of Japanese food has increased. In the early days, dishes commonly offered at Japanese restaurants were limited to several well-known Japanese foods: sukiyaki and tempura, for instance. Then, *teppanyaki* got popular as knife-wielding chefs prepared steak, seafood, and chicken entrees with soy-sauce flavoring right at guests' tables. Nowadays, sushi seems to have taken over the place of the most popular Japanese food in the United States. Food-business experts say that even *teppanyaki* restaurants can hardly attract diners unless they have a sushi bar.

The Japanese cuisine now being offered in the United States is diverse, ranging from traditional full-course *kaiseki* cuisine, a meal featuring small amounts of food of various textures and preparation methods, made to please the eye, too, to fusion foods.

Even "home-meal replacements" (HMRs), or ready-to-eat prepared meals, include a variety of Japanese food in their line-ups in order to expand their sales: for example, teriyaki *bentō* lunch packs, teriyaki chicken balls, and sushi packs have proved to be popular.

Moreover, the popularity of such Japanese foods as *soba* noodles, tofu and *kani-kamaboko*, or fish paste with crab flavor, as well as Japanese green tea, is growing among health-conscious Americans. They are used in fusion foods, too.

Moreover, Japanese food has been so popular that soy sauce, a traditional seasoning of Japan, and "instant" noodles, one of most distinguished inventions of postwar Japan, are available at virtually any supermarket in the United States. Sushi and other Japanese dishes are not part of regular meals of American families, but are specialties that people enjoy when they go out for dining. Instant noodles and such seasonings as soy sauce and teriyaki sauce are gradually becoming part of American home meals.

2. THE GROWING INTEREST IN JAPANESE CUISINE

How did Japanese cuisine make its way into the United States in the post-war period?

The export of Japanese foodstuffs to the United States, referred to in Japan as "pickled-radish trade," resumed in 1947, after years of suspension due to World War II. Two years later, in 1949, the General Headquarters (GHQ) of the Allied Forces in Tokyo approved the export of soy sauce.

In 1957, Kikkoman, a leading soy-sauce producer of Japan, established its sales company in San Francisco, seeking a new market in the United States. Years of efforts were devoted to cultivating interest in Japanese traditional seasoning, with the company hold tasting demonstrations at supermarkets and mobilizing home economists to develop recipes that were palatable to Americans.

Another producer of Japanese ethnic food, Nisshin Food Products, also was active in developing a market for its products in the United States.

Immediately after Nisshin developed instant Chinese-style noodles for the first time in the world in 1958, it started marketing its products both at home and in the United States simultaneously. The company's first job was to attract the interest of American foodstuff wholesalers who knew nothing about instant Chinese-style noodles. Then promotional campaigns were directed at general consumers. Thanks to painstaking efforts, Japanese "instant *ramen*" noodles were given space in supermarkets' dried-soup corners that once were dominated by major American manufacturers of soups. The marketing of instant Chinese-style noodles was successful, enabling the company to construct a plant to produce "Cup' o Noodles" in Los Angeles in 1973.

With the completion of its first U.S. plant, Nisshin developed a new marketing strategy for American consumers—to encourage them to switch from chopsticks to forks when eating noodles. In the United States, Nisshin promoted the use of forks instead of chopsticks for eating noodles The idea was simple but radical. In Japan in those days, nobody could imagine that noodles could be eaten with forks. The result of Nisshin's strategy was that instant Chinese-style noodles were accepted by Americans as part of their changing lifestyles.

In the restaurant-business field, Benihana of Tokyo opened its first restaurant on Fifth Avenue in New York City in 1964, when Tokyo hosted the Olympic Games. The Japanese steakhouse attracted American customers with a "samurai ceremony" by chefs and steaks having a soy-sauce flavor, although Japanese customers were reportedly puzzled by its steaks with bean sprouts. Benihana of Tokyo has since grown, and it now operates 64 restaurants across the United States. Of the 64, 40 reportedly have sushi bars. This restaurant chain greatly contributed to the promotion of soy sauce and chopsticks among Americans.

In 1961, Kikkoman developed teriyaki sauce, a soy-sauce-based new product that meets the tastes and lifestyles of American consumers. In 1973 it began producing both soy sauce and teriyaki sauce at its newly built plant in Wisconsin, from where it shipped the products to stores and restaurants across the United States.

Other soy-sauce manufacturers followed suit: Sanjirushi built a plant in Virginia in 1989, and in 1995 Yamasa began shipping soy sauce made in its Oregon plant. Meeting with the growing demand for this traditional Japanese seasoning, Kikkoman built its second U.S. plant in California and started shipping from there in 1998.

Japanese manufacturers of instant Chinese-style noodles were also active in developing the American market. Nisshin Food Products built three manufacturing plants, one each in California, Pennsylvania, and Tennessee. Toyo Suisan, after building a plant in California in 1977, built two more plants, one in Virginia and one in California.

Major brewers of saké or Japanese rice wine also made inroads into the U.S. market in the late 1970s and early 1980s. Their major targets were Japanese restaurants rather than American households.

Other Japanese manufacturers of ethnic foodstuffs, including boiled fish paste, vinegar, and tofu also jumped on the bandwagon, starting local production in the United States.

3. FUSION FOODS

In the 1980s, the Japanese way of management, including quality-control and personnel-management systems, attracted global attention. That was also the time that babyboomers, who account for more than 30 percent of the U.S. population, reached middle age.

Babyboomers became the mainstream of American consumers, setting trends in the market. Middle-aged babyboomers preferred a low-calorie and low-cholesterol diet. Many of them were members of dual-income families. They were well to do but often could not find time for cooking at home. They were open-minded regarding different cultures, contributing to the further diversification of American culinary cultures.

The Book of Tofu, by William Shurtleff and Akiko Aoyagi, was published, and a "tofu kit"—a wooden box and other ingredients for making tofu at home—was put on sale in the late 1970s. That book and tofu kit reportedly triggered a tofu boom in the United States, and babyboomers spearheaded it. Japanese-style tofu, unlike solid Chinese-style tofu, became widely available at grocery stores that offered Japanese foodstuffs among others.

Natural-food advocates started publicizing how to make and eat tofu at home. Shurtleff was among them. Unlike the Japanese traditional way of eating *hiyayakko,* or chilled tofu with bonito flakes, green onions, and squashed ginger, he instead recommended, among other suggestions, eating tofu with nuts, dried grapes, and honey. His recipes, which reflected his extensive knowledge of the nutritional value of soy beans, was nothing but a fusion of Japanese and American diets.

Under such circumstances, sushi has become a typical home-meal replacement, and sushi corners are now found at more than 30 percent of supermarkets in the United States, as Americans, who are becoming more and more health conscious, consume more fish.

In 1992, Teriyaki Boy, a Japanese-style take-out deli that turned out to be very popular, opened its first store, in Manhattan. Its HMRs were rated as nutritious, well-balanced, ready-made meals. In 1985, Yoshinoya West in Los Angeles introduced teriyaki chicken bowls to its menu of beef bowls. These, too, turned out to be very popular, thanks to the diet fads of those days.

In Japan, teriyaki refers to fish grilled with soy sauce and other seasonings. In the United States, it refers to barbecue beef or chicken cooked in that way. At supermarkets, teriyaki sauce has its own corner, separate from soy sauce, competing with tomato-based barbecue sauce. Teriyaki underwent a slight change in the United States, and an American-style teriyaki was created. The American version of teriyaki reflects a fusion of Japanese and American tastes.

In the United States, Japanese cuisine that makes the most of various ingredients has particularly attracted the interest of baby-boomers, because meat, fish, vegetables, grains, and other ingredients are well-balanced in the American diet. The fusion of Japanese and American foods was created by babyboomers, whose value systems are different from those of previous generations.

4. Conclusion

It is said that French cuisine is filled with extracts of ingredients, while in Japanese cuisine, which takes full advantage of ingredients' special qualities, soup stock plays a vital role.

After World War II, many Americans were exposed to different cultures, and their value systems have further diversified. Babyboomers in particular created new lifestyles. Under such circumstances, Japanese cuisine has been attracting American people and spreading across the United States because it is healthy, nutritionally well-balanced, and looks and tastes good.

Nevertheless, Japanese cuisine generally is eaten at restaurants or taken out from restaurants or supermarkets. It is not food that ordinarily is prepared at typical American homes. With the exception of instant noodles and soy sauce, it has not yet become part of the day-to-day home cooking of ordinary American households. Instant Chinese-style noodles, which were developed in Japan, typically are consumed as a snack food in American homes, and soy sauce is used in American home cooking.

The culinary cultures of Japan and the United States are blending, changing the two nations' dietary practices and traditional value systems, and creating a new wave of fusion foods. Such a fusion of culinary cultures also is affecting France, Italy, and Britain, leading to the creation of a new global culinary culture. At the beginning of the new millennium, we are facing great changes in food cultures.

JAPANESE CULTURE IN THE UNITED STATES   127

Rocky Aoki, *Jinsei shinumade chōsenda* (Tokyo: Tokyo Shimbun Shuppan-kyoku, 1989).

JETRO, *Jissen shokuhin yushutsu dokuhon* (Tokyo: JETRO, 2000).

Nobumasa Matsumoto, *Shōyu monogatari* (Tokyo: Kikkoman Corporation, 1976).

Ichirō Miura and Hiroshi Koezuka, *Nisshin Shokuhin no maneijimento* (Kyoto: Ritsumeikan University Keiei Senryaku Kenkyū Center, 1997).

Yūzaburō Mogi, *Shōyu ga America no shokutaku ni nobottahi* (Tokyo: PHP, 1983).

Yūzaburō Mogi, *Masatsunaki kokusaisenryaku* (Tokyo: Serunēto Shuppan, 1988).

Toshihisa Nagasaka, *Bebībūmā* (Tokyo: Simul Press, 1988).

Yoshiya Satō, *Fūmi wo uru otokotachi* (Tokyo: Recruit Shinsho, 1979).

Yoshinoya D and C, *Yoshinoya sōgyō 100-nenshi* (Tokyo: Yoshinoya, 1998).

Chapter 7

CONSISTENT JAPANESE, CHANGEABLE AMERICANS:

Japanese and American Attitudes toward Each Other in the Postwar Period

AKIRA IIKURA

INTRODUCTION

The feelings of Japanese and Americans toward each other have been more or less favorable since the end of the Pacific War. According to opinion polls conducted since the late 1970s, Japanese have consistently maintained favorable feelings toward the United States, although there has been some fluctuation. On the American side, as opinion polls conducted in the United States since 1960 show, views regarding Japan had been positive until the late 1980s, even though they have been susceptible to changes and fluctuations depending on the issues that arose on certain occasions. Indeed, in the late 1980s and early 1990s, the two countries' public opinion toward each other, especially American public opinion toward Japan, deteriorated. However, good feelings toward each other have again grown in recent years. The late 1990s might be regarded as a period in which the two nations held highly favorable sentiments toward each other. In this article I attempt to clarify how Japanese and Americans have felt toward each other in the postwar period by referring to public opinion polls conducted in both countries. In addition, I suggest what relationship would be most desirable for the two countries in the future. I believe that, in order to ease tensions when trouble arises, Japanese and Americans, which have the power to influence each other, should not only strengthen their economic and security ties, but should also more positively promote universal values such as democracy, respect for human rights, and freedom.

JAPANESE ATTITUDES TOWARD THE UNITED STATES

Japanese sentiments toward the United States have been stable and favorable throughout the postwar period. The Japanese people's good feelings toward the United States have prevailed for a long time, although some people—those who suffered from U.S. economic policies, and those who opposed the U.S.–Japan security treaty—sometimes had negative feelings toward the United States. Annual national surveys conducted between 1978 and 2000 and released by the Prime Minister's Office (Figure 1) show that more than 70 percent of the Japanese people had close or rather close feelings toward the United States during almost all those years. In contrast, the Japanese who didn't feel close to America never exceeded 30 percent during that 22-year period. It is interesting to note that even in the late 1980s and early 1990s, when anti-U.S. sentiments such as *kenbei*, dislike of America, were growing in Japan, the Japanese public-opinion polls didn't show a clear deterioration of pro-American feelings. For instance, the 1991 survey showed that 78 percent of the Japanese people had favorable feelings toward the United States. That figure was the highest of all those 22 years.

There is no country other than the United States for which the Japanese people have continued to feel favorably for more than 20 years. Why has the Japanese opinion of America been so stable and so favorable? Several reasons can be mentioned. In terms of national security, the United States has been the most important country for Japan, because it is Japan's only ally. Furthermore, the economic ties between the two countries have been very strong, despite the sometimes furious trade friction since the 1970s. In addition, Japanese culture has been overwhelmingly influenced by American culture in the postwar period. Although cultural pene-

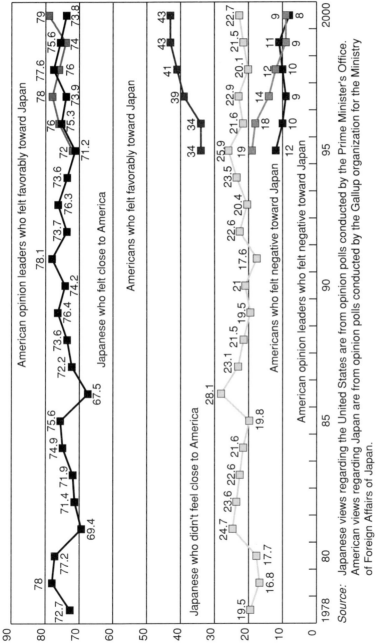

Source: Japanese views regarding the United States are from opinion polls conducted by the Prime Minister's Office. American views regarding Japan are from opinion polls conducted by the Gallup organization for the Ministry of Foreign Affairs of Japan.

Figure 1. Japanese and American Views of Each Other

tration tends to cause repulsion against it, American culture has tactfully infiltrated the Japanese way of life, even as it was in turn absorbing influences from Japan. Cultural exchanges between the two countries have also contributed to good feelings toward the United States.

The stability of Japanese sentiment toward the United States can also be attributed to the massive inflow of American information into Japan. From time to time there have been many news items from the United States that conveyed negative American views regarding Japan. Yet this has made the Japanese public inured to such unfavorable opinions. Even when Japanese people learn about anti-Japanese sentiments in the United States, they might think "That is America. There's no way to stop that." In other words, Japanese, through ample knowledge and information about the United States, have habituated themselves to American negative reactions.

Although the Japanese perception of the United States has remained positive for more than 20 years, public opinion polls don't necessarily reveal deep feelings. There was a very strong anti-U.S. movement around 1960, when the two countries concluded a new security treaty. As was clear in this case, in those days it was leftist people who were anti-America, while conservatives were pro-America. Leftists, pacifists, and politically aware citizens organized anti-Vietnam War movements and opposition to American policies in the later half of the 1960s and early 1970s. However, beginning in the mid-1980s, there were some changes, as some leading conservative figures in Japan began to express anti-American feelings. Although nationalism had never been advocated strongly in Japan after the Pacific War, there were signs of a resurgence of nationalism around the early 1990s. More important, just as earlier Japanese nationalism had stemmed from the impact of Western powers on Japan in the closing years of the Edo era, so the new nationalism seems to have stemmed in response to United States pressure on Japan. At that time, many Japanese thought that they were unfairly being blamed for America's economic failure over the past decade or so. Although the attitude of the Japanese public toward the United States was fundamentally favorable, as has been said, negative attitudes were growing among the Japanese people around 1990. However, that kind of anti-American nationalism seems not to have flourished in the later half of the 1990s. Furthermore, liberal people who had once bitterly criticized America's policies, such as that nation's Vietnam policy, have begun to positively assess the universal values, such as democracy, respect for the human rights, multiculturalism, and freedom, that have been advocated by the United States. The later half of 1990s have witnessed stable and highly favorable Japanese attitudes toward the United States.

AMERICAN ATTITUDES TOWARD JAPAN

U.S. sentiments toward Japan have been susceptible to change and fluctuation, depending on the issues that arose on various occasions. These sentiments ranged from initial indifference to admiration, and then to fear by the beginning of the 1990s. In the mid-1970s, the American attitude toward Japan was one of indifference. The U.S. media paid little attention to Japan. In the late 1970s, however, indifference changed to curiosity, and in the early 1980s that changed to admiration, because Americans were favorably impressed by Japan's remarkable economic recovery and the quality of this country's exported products. However, this favorable feeling didn't last long, due to the growing imbalance in U.S.–Japan bilateral trade and serious economic problems in the United States, such as the budgetary deficit of the U.S. government and growing unemployment. In the mid-1980s, admiration changed to apprehension. However, the negative attitudes toward Japan at that time were confined to a few American interest groups, such as organized labor, which attributed unemployment to foreign competition, and to a few American industries, which feared losing in competition with their Japanese counterparts. In the late 1980s, that apprehension turned to outright fear. A few people, mainly on Capitol Hill, attempted in the mid-1980s to generate anti-Japanese sentiment—an attempt largely ignored by the general public—and found themselves with a much broader base of "negative support" a few years later.

That trend was also reflected in yearly opinion polls conducted by the Gallup organization for the Ministry of Foreign Affairs of Japan (Figure 2). Americans who thought Japan was a dependable ally increased gradually from the 1960s to the mid-1980s, and Americans who regarded Japan as an unreliable ally began to decrease in the mid-1970s, although there were some fluctuations in these views. For example, the year 1974 showed a drastic 11-point drop due to Japan's pro-Arab policy during the energy crisis in the previous year. This revealed the changeable nature of U.S. public opinion. It can be said, however, that U.S. sentiments toward Japan had been positive until the mid-1980s. However, there appeared symptoms of the eroding of those positive sentiments in the late 1980s. A survey conducted in 1990 showed a considerable change in U.S. public opinion. According to the poll, 40 percent of Americans regarded Japan as an unreliable ally. The percentage holding that view was the highest since 1961, and it showed a drastic increase from the 29 percent of the previous year. In contrast, only 44 percent of Americans thought that Japan was a dependable ally. According to a *Business Week* poll in August 1989, as recited again and again, 68 percent of Americans considered the economic threat from Japan to be a more serious danger to the future of the United States than the military threat from the Soviet Union. This negative trend continued until 1994, when the percentage of Americans who regarded Japan as a dependable ally became 43 percent. That was equal to the percentage who didn't consider Japan to be a dependable ally.

Why did American sentiments deteriorate over those years? Actually, the late 1980s and early 1990s was not a good period for U.S.–Japan relations. America's enormous trade deficit with Japan didn't decline sufficiently. Feelings of frustration on the part of both nations resulted because of issues such as the controversial Structural Impediments Initiative (SII); overwhelming Japanese investment, as if "Japan is buying America"; Japan's insufficient contribution to resolving the Gulf crises and the Gulf War of 1990–91; and hard-going trade negotiations between the two nations. For many Americans, the cause of the deterioration was mainly economic problems.

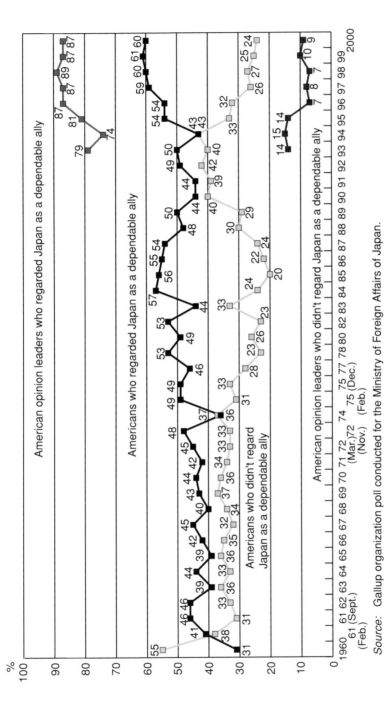

Source: Gallup organization poll conducted for the Ministry of Foreign Affairs of Japan.

Figure 2. Is Japan a Dependable Ally?

American views regarding Japan again began to turn favorable in 1995, and from 1997 to 2000 about 60 percent of Americans, the highest percentage for 40 years, regarded Japan as a dependable ally. In addition, Americans who considered Japan to be unreliable was less than 30 percent during those years. The later half of the 1990s might be recorded as a period of highly favorable U.S. feelings toward Japan. This has been attributed to the unprecedented economic boom in the United States and the easing of tensions that had been caused by economic friction. For example, 28 percent of those who in 1993 said that Japan was unreliable attributed the reason to Japan's trade policies, economic friction, and competition with the United States. However, in 2000 that view was held by only 6 percent. It is interesting to note that those who considered Japan dependable also pointed out the economic ties, Japanese investments, and good bilateral trade as reasons for their opinion. This clearly shows that economic interdependence between the United States and Japan sometimes causes frictions, but that it also is indeed a ground of the good bilateral relations that exist between the two countries.

WHAT IS DESIRABLE?

What kind of relationship is desirable between the United States and Japan? In the later half of the 1990s, both nations perceived their bilateral relations as either excellent or good, and they felt favorable or close toward each other. Although press coverage in the two countries still sometimes oversimplifies issues, reinforces stereotypes, promotes misunderstandings, and, as a result, more or less distorts the relationship, in both countries the general public has recently showed stable favorable feelings toward the other country. No one thinks that the United States and Japan are on a collision course. However, their bilateral relations will be tested not in times of peace but when troubles arise. What is important is that the two countries maintain friendly relations even when their interests conflict with each other. Indeed, much learning can take place through controversy. It is necessary for both countries not only to strengthen their security and economic ties, but also to reconfirm in times of controversy that they share universal values such as democracy, freedom, and respect for human rights. If both Japanese and Americans can do that, it will be possible to resolve economic or security problems and other difficulties without considerably distorting their nations' bilateral relations.

Chapter 8

AMERICA AND ME

50 Years of the Japan–U.S. Relationship and Me

YASUHIRO NAKASONE

I first came into contact with Americans in 1941, during World War II, when U.S. B-17 warplanes fiercely bombed us as we were fighting to take the airfield near Davao in Mindanao, the Philippines. I was a two-year active-duty lieutenant in the Imperial Japanese Navy, and I took part as a Seabee paymaster. After Japan's defeat, in the capacity of a member of the Diet I submitted a proposal regarding occupation policy to General Douglas MacArthur and met with John Foster Dulles when he came to Tokyo to negotiate the peace treaty. Throughout those extraordinary times, many changes took place in me, because I was impressed with the humane attitude of American soldiers and U.S. support for our emperor system.

My consistent belief as a politician during the more than 50 post-war years of Japan's relations with the United States has been that despite the inevitable bright and dark sides of real politics, Japan's sympathy with and acceptance of America's ideals of freedom, democracy, peace, and human rights have contributed greatly to Japan, the United States, Asia, and the world—and have enriched my life as well. Because as a politician I have worked hard to help Japan recover its national strength and international status, I believe that but for the friendly help of the United States Japan would not be enjoying what it enjoys today, particularly in the areas of national security, peaceful use of atomic energy, the supply of petroleum and other natural resources, and international trade.

During my political life, the Americans who impressed me most strongly have included Edwin Reischauer, Henry Kissinger, Ronald Reagan, George Bush, and Robert Kennedy, all of whom addressed the people of the world with their American hearts and minds and showed the people of the world what America was.

In the latter half of the 20th century, the United States took the lead in successfully meeting the historic challenge of the West's Cold War with the Soviet Union. Now, at the outset of the 21st century, I hope that Washington will resolve America's outstanding issues with Beijing in a peaceful and friendly manner.

The United States is the sole military superpower remaining in the world. It is America that protects justice and human rights by sending its armed forces to many parts of the world, thereby serving to deter aggression and to maintain peace. This U.S. presence, if overemphasized, can lead to unilateral action, while if underutilized, to protectionism and isolationism. It is my fervent desire that in the 21st century, too, the United States will remain what it is today—the America that enjoys the trust and esteem of the world.

(Former Prime Minister)

*   *   *

My First Visit to the United States

KIICHI MIYAZAWA

I first went to the United States at the age of 19 to take part in an annual Japanese–American student conference, in which students of the two countries, male and female, traveled the country together during the summer vacation and took turns inviting each other to hold discussions on a college campus. That year, 1939, the conference was held at the University of Southern California.

At that time, because the war between Japan and China had been going on for more than two years and Japan's aggression was being roundly denounced by the international community, we Japanese students felt that our immediate task was to speak in defense of our country. Every day on the deck of the ship during the two-week voyage to the United States our group of nearly 50 students practiced arguing the case for Japan. Right after our ship, the *Kamakura Maru*, sailed from Yokohama, we received the news that the United States notified Japan that it had scrapped the nation's bilateral commerce and navigation treaty.

It was against this tense backdrop that the meeting at U.S.C. began. But instead of the Japanese and American students facing each other contentiously, they all mingled together, and many Americans criticized their own country and expressed sympathy with resource-poor Japan. The occasion thus turned out to be quite different from what we had anticipated on the ship—that we would have to play the role of defense attorneys for our country. We sensed that perhaps the Americans represented democracy in action, and we felt relieved after being uptight at the outset. But being young and flexible as we were, we quickly shared and discussed among ourselves the awe and fear that we felt—

that we wouldn't have a chance to win a war against the likes of our hosts.

We stayed with American families, and the head of my host family was a corporate executive. His house, which had lawns and a pool, was a place that the Japanese would call a mansion. Given such a gap in per-capita wealth between the two nations, I thought again that it would not be good for Japan to wage war with America. In the morning following the overnight stay, in order to have a wash I turned on the faucet marked "H," not knowing exactly what "H" meant. Hot water came out. Surprised, I said, "Hot water came from the H faucet," to a host-family member, who looked as puzzled at what I had said as if I had spoken incomprehensible English.

(Former Prime Minister)

*   *   *

My Relationship with the United States

YOSHIO OKAWARA

In 1951, I went to the United States for the first time, as a GAR-IOA (Government Appropriation for Relief in Occupied Areas) student. I studied there for 10 months. Coming from war-ravaged Japan, I was struck by the vast country, by its affluence, and, above all, by the depth of its people. It was a shining America in its golden age.

My first assignment at the Japanese Embassy in Washington, where I was counselor for economic affairs under Ambassador

Ryūji Takeuchi, extended for two years beginning in July 1963. As soon as I arrived at my post, I became busy dealing with the introduction of the U.S. interest-equalization tax. The assassination of President John F. Kennedy in November 1963 gave me the shock of my life. Then, with President Lyndon B. Johnson's continuation of U.S. involvement in Vietnam, I realized that American society was undergoing great changes.

My second tour of duty in Washington was from February 1971 to the summer of 1972, as a minister to assist Ambassador Nobuhiko Ushiba. Soon after the United States and Japan reached agreement on the return of Okinawa, the two so-called "Nixon Shocks" hit, the first being Henry Kissinger's secret visit to Beijing in July 1971, and the second the following month involving the decision to take the dollar off the gold standard. In the background, it seemed, lay President Richard Nixon's distrust of Japan following the textile trade dispute and an emotional gap between the White House and the State Department.

In 1972, I was appointed director-general of the American Affairs Bureau of the Foreign Ministry. I was charged with tackling the aftermath of the Nixon Shocks and issues concerning the activity of the U.S. forces in Japan in relation to the Vietnam War, which was sinking the United States deeper into a quagmire. Among those issues was the decision to make Yokosuka the home port for the U.S. aircraft carrier Midway.

From 1980 to 1985, after an ambassadorship to Australia, I served as ambassador to the United States. At the time of my arrival in Washington, the administration of President Jimmy Carter faced many difficulties, including a stagnant U.S. economy following the second oil crisis and diminished national prestige by the occupation of the U.S. Embassy in Iran, when its staff members were taken hostage. As the Cold War intensified, the United States put strong pressure on Japan to increase its defense spending.

With the advent of President Ronald Reagan's administration, the economy turned for the better, thanks to "Reaganomics," and the then-existing somber mood in the United States gave way to rising confidence in a strong America and a strong dollar. The United States, in opposition to "the Evil Empire," the Soviet Union, continued to hope for and to press for Japan's enhanced defense cooperation, but it began to use discretion and to avoid blatant pressure.

The U.S. government, concerned about the worsening trade imbalance with Japan, pursued a policy calling for free and fair trade. Thanks to the United States' good negotiating partner, U.S. Trade Representative William E. Brock, Japan agreed to voluntarily restrict its automobile exports in a way that was profitable to Japanese auto makers without eroding the principle of free trade. Agreements were also reached on raising the ceilings on beef and citrus imports from the United States. Subsequent major developments against the backdrop of the U.S. initiative to open Japan's doors to more American goods and services included the market-oriented sector-specific (MOSS) talks and the establishment of the bilateral working group to improve the yen-dollar exchange rate.

After I left Washington, discussions concerning Japan as a threat and as a "different" country arose in the latter half of the 1980s. It should be noted that a mutual perception gap between Japan and the United States remained a serious problem from the 1970s onward, amid the swelling U.S. trade deficit with Japan year after year as Japan's competitiveness grew.

(Former Ambassador to the United States)

*   *   *

Gifts of Peace

SHŌICHIRŌ TOYODA

I was 20 years old when World War II ended on August 15, 1945. I had been born in the year when the Showa era began. On the day of Japan's surrender I was home in Kosai City, Shizuoka Prefecture, on leave from the Toyota foundry where I had been working as a trainee until the previous week. The foundry had been bombed the day before, but fortunately nobody had been hurt, because the workers had been forewarned of the attack and had evacuated the facility. At home, sitting straight in a swept-out *tatami*-floor room with my mother, I heard Emperor Showa announce on the radio that he had accepted the Potsdam Declaration.

Although the war was over, our neighbors in the village fled to the mountains in a tumult, fearing possible acts of atrocity that the oncoming occupation forces might commit. My family lifted *tatami* mats and hid foodstuffs under the floor.

At 32 years of age, I set foot on American soil for the first time. I have never studied in the United States, nor have I stayed in one place there for more than one week, even though I have visited the country many times. Although I have no close personal ties with America, during a long and broad business relationship I have enjoyed both moral and material guidance and support from that country and its people. These are indeed gifts of peace, and I greatly appreciate them.

Japan and the United States together account for 40 percent of the world economy, and ties between the two countries are the most important of all the bilateral relationships in the international community. Cooperation between the two countries is important not only to the countries themselves, but also for the development of the world as a whole.

Whereas the main objective of the A50 Project is to express appreciation for the assistance rendered by the United States and its people in the reconstruction of postwar Japan, I believe that we should not be content with lavishing praise on America out of comparison between our country and others. I believe that our true purpose is to promote peace in every corner of the entire world, and that this project is a part of that effort. I note that there still are Americans who ask where in China Japan is located. We have a long way to go to achieve true international understanding.

(Honorary Chairman, member of the Board of
Toyota Motor Corporation)

*   *   *

The Cole Family and My Experience of America

YŌTARŌ KOBAYASHI

It was after World War II that I first came into contact with the United States and its people.

Soon after the war's end, a U.S. Air Force officer, a certain Major Cole, and his family came to live in our neighborhood. Mrs. Cole, a tall, strikingly beautiful woman, was of Mexican extraction. The Coles had three children, who were a bit younger than my siblings and me. My gregarious mother first made friends with Mrs. Cole, and the other members of both families quickly followed suit. My father, who spoke English well, helped to bring the two families close to each other. Born in the Meiji era, he had a career in a trading house and had stayed a long time in London when he was young.

The Coles moved to Washington Heights, a U.S. military residential area in Yoyogi, Tokyo, that was closed to the Japanese public. They would treat us to giant steaks and overflowing heaps of ice cream in the officers' restaurant. That was very pleasing to us growing children—my younger brother and sister and myself.

Thereafter I fast became attracted to things American, through my baseball heroes Ted Williams and Bob Feller, film idols Elizabeth Taylor and Lana Turner, and my favorite authors William Faulkner and Mickey Spillane, whose translated works I read at random.

After graduating from a university in Japan, I immediately proceeded to the Wharton School of the University of Pennsylvania, where I managed to get an M.B.A. degree. I then returned to Japan and worked for Fuji Photo Film for five years before joining Fuji Xerox, a joint U.S.–Japanese company, in 1963. I have been with the latter company ever since, and obviously what I am I owe in part to my ties with the United States.

Revelations abounded in my American experience. While I was a student in the United States, by accident I learned that Major Cole has copiloted the lead plane of J. H. Doolittle's strike force of B-25 bombers that conducted the first air raid on Japan in 1942. In 1977, with my wife I attended for the first time an Aspen Institute seminar on classics, where I was made to realize how frivolously I had dismissed American executives as having few concerns beyond their company's quarterly corporate profits.

The United States, including its spectacular economic recovery and superpower performance over the past two decades, continues to be a source of revelations and stimulation to me. I am sure that this will hold true in the future as well.

(Chairman of the Board, Fuji Xerox Co., Ltd.)

*   *   *

My First Experience in the United States

YOSHIHIKO MIYAUCHI

Of the many memories I have of the United States, that of my first encounter with Americans remains indelibly imprinted on my mind to this day. When World War II ended, I was a 10-year-old fourth-grader living in the countryside, to where I had been evacuated. I remember a few national elections that were held as democracy was emerging in Japan from the confusion following the nation's defeat. Each time an election was held, three or four young American soldiers of the Occupation Forces came by jeep to the rural town hall to monitor the poll, and each time my father was asked by the town authorities to serve as an interpreter for a few days for those soldiers.

Father made friends with them, and we invited the Americans to our humble—by today's standard—country home, where they enjoyed themselves over saké and sukiyaki that was made with specially rationed beef. They were the first Americans I came into contact with. Watching them talking freely with my father and drinking in such a cheerful mood, I said to myself, "How happy they are! I should learn to understand the mysterious language they are speaking."

The soldiers drove my sister and me around town on their jeep, much to our delight. I was deeply impressed with their outgoing demeanor and the language they spoke, of which at first I did not understand even one word.

Since then, I have been to the United States many times, first as a student and then on business, making an increasing number of friends and acquaintances there. My positive feeling toward the sunny, outgoing character of many Americans and the cultural climate of the country that they have created has remained unchanged to this day.

The English language remains a formidable challenge to me, and I have yet to have a good command of it, despite years of study. I am still struggling to communicate well in English, and sometimes I feel frustrated because of my inadequacy in that regard.

Strikingly, my perception of America today has little changed from that which I had when I was a child. The upbeat friendliness that those American soldiers conveyed to a boy of a defeated enemy country right after the war still captivates me.

(Chairman and Chief Executive Officer of ORIX Corporation)

* * *

America: A Nation of Equal Opportunities

HANAE MORI

Looking back on the postwar period, when I began to work as a fashion designer, it was in New York that I took my first step toward expanding my activities worldwide. America extended a hand of welcome to me, an obscure young designer from Japan. I was one of those who benefited from the generosity with which the

United States supported Japan's postwar reconstruction and accepted diverse and possibly talented people from its former enemy.

I flew to New York and Los Angeles for the first time in 1961, when many Japanese, steeped in American culture, looked upon the United States as a symbol of modernity. Curiosity about this giant neighbor on the other side of the Pacific prompted me to cross that ocean, where I found a sunny nation of abundance, freedom, and a melting pot of races.

A friend of mine introduced me to Oleg Cassini, then the chief designer for Jacqueline Kennedy, who was at the height of fashion. At his showroom, Cassini personally poured me coffee and showed me his preshipment collection. A garment-maker executive even invited me to work for him. This presented a striking contrast to what I experienced when I visited Paris during the winter of that same year.

Determined to test my mettle in an environment hospitable to new things and new, hopefully promising, faces, I held my first New York show in 1965. I was lucky enough, in a country that is candid about "yes" and "no," to get on the "yes" escalator.

I have learned much from competitive America. And with the help of friends and acquaintances there, since I set up shop in Paris I have continued my work until today. My sense of gratitude is the source of my energy to devote myself to the A50 Project to further develop Japan–U.S. relations. I will do what I can to contribute to the success of this effort.

(Fashion designer)

＊　　＊　　＊

Fond Remembrances of America

Yukio Matsuyama

When I was assigned to Washington for the first time as a corre-
spondent of the *Asahi Shimbun* (newspaper) 40 years ago, I asked
a State Department official dealing with Far Eastern affairs if he
knew of an American family that would rent me a room so that I
could get crash training in English conversation for six months
before my wife and daughter came to join me. The official immediately took me to an apparently upper-middle-class home, where
I was met a lady, who spoke refined English, and her two daughters
met me. I liked them at once and moved from the hotel where I had
been staying to live with them. It turned out that her husband was
an outstanding mathematician, she a devout Quaker, and the whole
family of an ultra-serious type.

Living in a Quaker home gave me one surprise after another,
because I had had an education that can be termed either liberal or
loose, and I was used to a hurried, restless life as a reporter back in
Japan. My preconceived notion, which had been nurtured by
Hollywood movies, of a mammonistic, hedonistic America was
shattered. I fondly remember an argument regarding the rent: the
lady of the house insisted on $10 a week, and I was adamant about
my offer of $20. The State Department official intervened in the
end, and we compromised on $15 a week.

Through this family, it was hammered into me that the essentials
of the American spirit were to be found among the 13 virtues
exhorted by Benjamin Franklin. These included diligence, thrift,
moderation, modesty, cleanliness, and fidelity. As a result, the idea
that the United States was fundamentally sound became the
bedrock of my outlook on the country, remaining even when I

wrote articles about the cruelty and callousness of politics dominated by lawyers and military people, and about the dark side of society, contaminated by crime and drugs.

It still puzzles me that my American host family, which included no Japanophile and had no habit of eating sushi nor any knowledge of *kabuki* or Yukio Mishima, should have been so kind to a strange Japanese boarder. The lady of the house treated my wife with affection, as if my wife were her own daughter, and she treated my older daughter like her own grandchild. When my second daughter was born in a hospital in Virginia, our American hostess was the first to visit there, and she even agreed to be the godmother of the baby, a relationship that she has proudly remembered ever since.

After we returned to Tokyo, members of my family visited her whenever they happened to be in the United States. Although her husband died more than a decade ago, the lady, still full of vitality at 92 years of age, devotes herself to social service. That the likes of this lady—whom we can call the salt of the earth—are found everywhere in American society seems to underscore that country's strength and glamour.

(Former Chief Editorial Writer of the Asahi Shimbun)

*   *   *

In Appreciation of
Milk Supplied by LARA

KYŌKO TABATA

When I was about to get married 30 years ago, my mother gave me an old empty can and yellowed baby underwear and said, "This can contained milk that sustained your life." I was born in August 1947, when, my mother told me, she could not breastfeed me because she was undernourished. Her request for milk rations was refused, and my father was averse to buying anything on the black market. But while my mother was burdened with a crying baby in her arms, she received some LARA (Licensed Agencies for Relief in Asia) milk from a convent. "Seeing you grow, I became so touched by this can that I couldn't throw it away," my mother told me.

When I was a child, I heard about LARA supplies, but I was unaware of the details about who sent them and why and how, except that they had come from the United States and Canada. To a juvenile mind they were gifts full of good will.

It seems that references to World War II were somehow avoided in the school education that my generation received. About 40 years after the end of the war, people began to discuss it from different angles, reflecting the affluent society, changing international relations, and freedom of information that characterized Japan at that time. I had been doing my own thinking, in terms of both being a victim and a perpetrator, when I read a book by Kuniji Shimbori about George Ernest Bott, a Canadian missionary. It reminded me of the empty can I had all but forgotten, because I learned that Reverend Bott was the director of LARA, which, according to the book, benefited 14 million Japanese for seven years beginning in the autumn of 1946.

Many of us have lived the more than 50 years of the postwar period without reflecting on the nature of LARA supplies, perhaps because we were too impoverished to do so in a war-torn country when we were receiving them. I did not know that our first Miss Japan contest was held so as to choose a goodwill envoy to carry a message of thanks for the LARA relief. I also did not know that many Japanese residents and their offspring in North America contributed enthusiastically to sending the supplies, or that numerous citizens in the United States and Canada devoted themselves to bringing this humanitarian program into reality.

When my second daughter spent a year in a small town in Washington State as a high school exchange student five years ago, I let her take with her the photograph of the empty milk can that I had kept, in order for her to convey my thanks to the people there if she had an opportunity to speak in public. Her sponsoring parents told me in a letter that she gave a speech and impressed the audience.

As I renew my appreciation of the LARA relief that supported my life, I remember once again the spirit with which it was extended to us. The generation that survived on relief milk and became able to a smile again is beginning to have grandchildren. I hope that we, together with this succeeding generation and others to follow, will become a humanely developed nation.

(Housewife)

✳   ✳   ✳

My Friendship with Bob Orr

Hirotsugu Iikubo

I graduated from DePauw University, in the State of Indiana, in 1957. DePauw has had a long history with Japan, first enrolling four Japanese students in 1876. One of these became an outstanding Japanese Ambassador to America. In addition, my late father was also a graduate.

In the summer of 1993, I had the privilege of inviting Robert Orr, former governor of Indiana and former American Ambassador to Singapore, to my home for dinner. At that time he said, "When I was governor, unemployment was a big issue in Indiana, and there was a Japanese automobile manufacturer that built a plant to help solve this problem, and I still feel grateful for this. Ever since then, as an expression of my personal appreciation, I have owned cars made by that company."

It dawned on me at that moment that we Japanese had overlooked the importance of expressing thanks, in a visible form, for the enormous and crucial assistance given to us during the time of our recovery immediately after the war. Although this unprecedented American gesture could also have been part of that nation's global strategy, I felt there was a need for the Japanese people to show their dignity by expressing their appreciation for this very important assistance.

The former West Germany, Italy, and the citizens of Berlin have all recognized their obligation to express their thanks to the United States in a visible manner. It is said that Korea is planning a major event for 2003, to commemorate the 50th year since the end of the Korean War. In addition, China is practicing its tradition of not forgetting those responsible for having had a major impact in its favor.

In view of this common worldwide practice, it would be no exaggeration to say that Japan's failure to visible express its gratitude is out of line with accepted international principles.

I have wanted to start a specific project to demonstrate to America how much we Japanese as a people who value common sense and dignity, feel an obligation to visibly express our thanks. I have met with many leaders, from all areas of society, and I held forty-four meetings prior to the Official Promoters Meeting in May of 1998, where Ambassador Yoshio Okawara was elected as the chairperson, thus launching our activities as an organization.

My friendship with Ambassador Orr triggered the start of this movement, and I am most thankful to all those people who contributed their efforts towards the fruition of the A50 project. I hope that this will be the beginning of initiating A50 Phase 2, as well as other activities, by the youth of both countries, perhaps on an even-wider scale.

(Chairman and CEO of Decision Systems Inc.)

REMARKS CONCERNING THE A50 PROJECTS

The occupation policy and attitude shown by America towards Japan was extraordinarily mild and magnanimous, well beyond the scope of treatment that the vanquished might expect from their victors. Although the Japanese themselves have worked diligently to bring about the recovery of their country from devastation, one should never forget the enormous support and cooperation extended to the Japanese people by America in the form of humanitarian aid, contributions to our industrial recovery, the modernization of our society, and providing a huge free market for Japanese products.

The idea of A50 ("A" standing for appreciation and America, and "50" for the past 50 years, 50 states, and the next 50 years) began with the firm desire to express gratitude to America for its exceptional benevolence towards the Japanese people during the postwar period, to review and reassess the amicable 50 years of U.S.–Japan relations since then, and to help further strengthen this mutual-trust relationship. Good U.S.–Japan relations have been supported not only by the governments involved, but by large numbers of people of both nations who value nurturing and promoting mutual trust and a strong sense of cooperation. A50 is a grass-roots movement that was initially conceived of by Hirotsugu Iikubo, chairman of the A50 Steering Committee, to help further strengthen this relationship. There are many people who share the same sentiments and who have worked on various committees as volunteers to make the success of this project a reality.

We are delighted that one of the results of this project is the publication of this book, a historical review of the past 50 years since the signing of the peace treaty. It also provides a record of the post-Treaty Occupation period, which has influenced Japan's political, diplomatic, economic, and social perspectives so greatly. At the same time, the aim of this book is to focus on the positive partnership aspects of U.S.–Japan relations. The writers who contributed to this book come from academia, business, social organizations, and other relevant areas, and some of its contents are in narrative form, to be enjoyed by everyone.

We would like to thank the individuals and corporations that have financially supported this cause despite the current sluggish economy. This book could not have been completed without the efforts of these public-spirited people and organizations. The originally planned activities of the A50 project will be completed at a 50th Commemoration of the Signing of the Treaty ceremony, but it is our strong hope and resolve to have this spirit of A50 carried on, in whatever form, by the youth of our two great nations.

A50 Executive Committee

July 2001

AFTERWORD

This book is in part an abridged translation of a Japanese book titled *Nihon to America: pātonāshippu no 50-nen*, which will be published by the Japan Times, Ltd. simultaneously with this work. This volume contains some chapters that are essentially the same as the essays written for that Japanese book, but it also includes chapters that contain new material written especially for this English version.

The book consists of eight chapters. The first chapter, written by Tadashi Aruga on the basis of an essay in Japanese by him and three other writers—Chihiro Hosoya, Osamu Ishii, and Akira Iikura—illuminates postwar U.S.–Japan relations primarily in regard to diplomatic, political, and security developments. This chapter not only constitutes a good introduction to the postwar history of the two countries' relationship, but also makes it clear that this postwar bilateral relationship has on the whole been beneficial to both nations, particularly for Japan.

Chapter two, which is an abridged translation of Nagayo Honma's original essay in the Japanese volume, describes how postwar Japanese society and culture have been "Americanized." This does not mean, however, that Japan has become a "little America," but rather, as Honma explains, that Japan has integrated American culture into its own. In this regard, the Americanization of Japanese culture has proceeded in tandem with the "Japanization" of American culture.

Chapter four, written by Masako Iino, deals with the history of Japanese Americans after World War II. It vividly describes how their status has been influenced by the relationship between the two countries and how Japanese Americans have been concerned about conditions in Japan. What should be noted here is that Japanese Americans played a significant role in aiding starving Japanese people during the occupation period.

Chapters three and six are abridged translations of the original Japanese essays, which discuss how Japanese companies made inroads into U.S. markets after the war. In chapter three, Kōichi Shimokawa explains how Japanese manufacturers, especially food, electric, and automobile companies, started production in the United States and infused their Japanese-style production systems into their local U.S. operations. He points out how Japanese-style management played a role in the revival of American companies, especially of the "Big Three" auto manufacturers in the 1990s. However, as indicated in both chapters three and six, not only Japanese vehicles and electrical devices, but also Japanese foods, gained footholds in U.S. markets. In chapter six, Yūzaburō Mogi explains how Japanese cuisine began to appeal to American people, spread across the United States, and became part of American home meals.

Chapter five, written by Akiko Kuno. discusses how contributions of Japan–America societies helped to promote mutual understanding between the two countries after the war. Kuno describes how the societies' various activities, including educational and cultural exchange programs, have helped to build trust between the peoples of the two countries.

The growing mutual trust between Japanese and Americans is also discussed in chapter seven, written by Akira Iikura, who examines how the two peoples have felt toward each other since the end of the Pacific War. Referring to opinion polls conducted in both countries during the past few decades, he states that Japanese sentiments toward the United States have been stable and favorable since the 1980s, while those of Americans toward Japan have sometimes fluctuated, though the late 1990s witnessed highly favorable feelings by both peoples toward the other.

Chapter eight, the last chapter, focuses on 10 Japanese people's personal feelings of friendship towards the United States. It comprises short essays written by contributors who include two former prime ministers of Japan, leading figures in diplomacy, business, and culture, and so-called ordinary citizens. Although it is difficult to summarize their diverse views, it can be said that they have maintained favorable attitudes toward the United States and its people, even if in some respect they experienced difficulty with regard to that country.

As Tadashi Aruga stresses in the last part of his essay, it was truly fortunate for Japan to be democratized after the war. Although the postwar peace and prosperity of Japan should be attributed mainly to the efforts of Japanese people themselves, it should be remembered that it was America that helped Japan to return to the international community as a liberal democratic nation, to prosper as the world's second-largest capitalist economy, and to enjoy unbroken peace for the more than 50 years that have passed since the end of World War II.

A50 Editorial Committee

Contributors

Editor

Chihiro HOSOYA
Professor Emeritus,
International University of Japan;
Professor Emeritus,
Hitotsubashi University

A50 Editorial Committee

Chihiro HOSOYA
Tadashi ARUGA
Ken KONDO
Makoto MASUI
Masahiko YAMANE
Akira IIKURA

AUTHORS

Chapter 1
Tadashi ARUGA
Professor, Seigakuin University;
Professor Emeritus,
Hitotsubashi University

Chapter 2
Nagayo HONMA
Chancellor, Seijo Gakuen;
Professor Emeritus,
University of Tokyo

Chapter 3
Kōichi SHIMOKAWA
Professor, Tokaigakuen University;
Professor Emeritus, Hosei University

Chapter 4
Masako IINO
Professor, Tsuda College

Chapter 5
Akiko KUNO
Executive Director,
The America–Japan Society, Inc.

Chapter 6
Yūzaburō MOGI
President and CEO, Kikkoman
Corporation

Chapter 7
Akira IIKURA
Associate Professor,
Josai International University

TRANSLATORS

Ayako DOI
Editor, Japan Digest
Translated and summarized chapters 2
and 5.

Takeshi HIKINO
Professor, Konan Women's University;
Former Managing Editor,
Mainichi Daily News
Translated and summarized chapters 3
and 6.

Hajime SEKI
Former New York Bureau Chief,
Mainichi Newspapers
Translated chapter 8, except IIKUBO's
essay.

201